The Quest for Fitness

The Quest for Fitness

A rational exploration into the new science of organization

Mark Michaels

Writers Club Press

San Jose New York Lincoln Shanghai

The Quest for Fitness
A rational exploration into the new science of organization

Writers Club Press
an imprint of iUniverse.com, Inc.

For information address:
iUniverse.com, Inc.
5220 S 16th, Ste. 200
Lincoln, NE 68512
www.iuniverse.com

ISBN: 0-595-18133-3

Printed in the United States of America

To my father, Abraham, who takes my iconoclasm in stride.

Contents

Introduction

Why science? Scientific management was a tool at the beginning of the 20th century. Our perception is that it did not work. It was too inhuman.

There are two answers. First, we use science to understand organizations because it is the only systematic approach to understanding available. We also use science because it does work.

Science, at its core, is the systematic search for an understanding of our world. It has progressed over time by replicating findings in an effort to prove what is not true. Each subsequent finding in science helps us understand our world a bit more as it removes more of our false perceptions. However, this process of dis-proval never allows us to stop searching. There are limits to this methodology, which, as the scientist John Casti[1] and others have explained, makes it impossible to answer all the questions.

The scientific process existed long before the notion of science. Stories exemplifying the scientific method can be found in the philosophical and theological arguments of different cultures. The Eastern symbols of the lotus blossom and the seven veils each represent the process of removing—disproving—misperceptions. In Judaism there are many tales of the great Rabbis, 2000 years ago, trying to understand God by discussing the laws against mentioning His names. Following

---

1 Casti, John L. *Paradigms Lost: Images of man in the mirror of science.*

these arguments of what He is not is just as rigorous as listening to a theorem proof in a chemistry lecture.

The scientific method can be found on a more fundamental level as well. Methodologies emerging from complex systems theory demonstrate that the process of dis-confirmation emerges from each culture's struggle for survival. The difference is only in the tools used and the amount of past knowledge that can be applied to the search process.

The relationship of these methods to the scientific method contradicts the new age and irrational notion that science is just one of several equally valid ways to understand reality. Rather than being its own way of knowing, science is recognized as the fundamental operation for extracting the real from the unreal that we always seem to confront.

It turns out that science is the best tool for developing effectiveness in organizations. The only drawback is that its usefulness is limited by the amount of scientific knowledge available at a given point in time. For instance, in the 17th century, science underwent a revolution resulting from the research of Sir Isaac Newton and others. The laws of motion and gravity, the discovery that the universe did not center on the Earth and the development of calculus all removed a series of untruths from our thinking. Two hundred years later, these changes became the foundation for the Industrial Revolution.

Application of traditional scientific thinking to organizations reached its pinnacle with the publication of Frederick Taylor's works on scientific management. Taylor created a production/management system based on the metaphor of an organization running like a clock. This was the same metaphor that emerged from Newton's work as the predominant description of the functioning of the Universe. In Taylorism, people fit into the system as physical parts—as cogs in the wheel of production.

Taylorism is alive and well, today. The latest applications of this "linear" thinking can be seen in re-engineering, statistical process control, ISO 9000, Motorola's Six Sigma quality processes, and the Baldrige awards. These and similar programs work, at least to a point. *The Quest for Fitness* will explore this limit in scientific management, and identify rational ways to surpass that limit.

Since the 1960s, rationality has become a casualty of the limit of Newtonian science. The limits of Newtonian theory were translated into organizational theory to mean that there would always be something missing in this scientifically established management system. The clock never stayed on time, the precision was always off, so managers should make their own time.

This unpredictability of human behavior forced us to adjust our thinking by adding a sense of humanism into management. To insert the human into an equation meant to add irrationality.

Some humanism worked, some didn't. It was possible to verify which processes were effective, but a satisfactory understanding of why only some of the strategies worked never emerged. Without a unifying theory, we could never build on our successes.

The ultimate attempt at a humanistic approach to management was "empowerment." However, empowerment never quite fit into organizational reality. Even if the clock had become warped, the leader continued as the clock maker. S/he could never really be able to give up power. A conflict existed between holding power to control chaos and the chaos that is implied in true empowerment. So long as this paradox exists, organizational theory is ripe for such irrational strategies.

The separation between rationality and science grew out of an apparent paradox between two major scientific themes of the 20th Century, relativity theory and quantum mechanics. Albert Einstein dedicated his later years to resolving this clash, with no success. Eventually, the existence of the paradox was interpreted to mean that reality is literally in the eye of the beholder. The thesis stated that comprehension of the universe is dependent upon the position of the observer (relativity) and that observation affects the status of the universe (quantum). The paradox led to a sort of narcissistic existentialism that proposed that one's reality was the fantasy of one's mind.

Management theorists translated this myth into a model of entrepreneurism in which the successful leader is portrayed as the builder of his or her world. Management theorists from Tom Peters to Margaret Wheatley created a pantheon of entrepreneurial heroes from Lee Iaccoca to Bill Gates. The mythological story prescribing the path to success was one of personal triumph through molding of one's environment. There is noting rational about this explanation of the new science of organizations.

The fallacy of this non-rational thinking has always been visible to anyone wishing to peer under the covers of the purported research. Those understanding statistics could see that the mythology was based mostly on anecdotal evidence. Research design remains very important to those who practice the strategies of scientific inquiry. Studies such as those of Tom Peters' "Excellent Companies" included fundamental research design flaws. In that case in particular, there was no attempt to determine what percent of failing company leaders followed the same prescriptions as those who were succeeding. With the publication of Peters' book, *The Circle of Innovation: You Can Shrink Your Way to Greatness,* we have reached the ultimate statement of irrationality in organizational theory.

The Quest for Fitness is an attempt to return rationality back to the scientific study of organizations. It starts by reawakening the scientific search for a rational understanding of our world.

Science has gone beyond Newton's clockwork universe over the past one hundred and fifty years. Newton studied all systems as if they functioned in a linear fashion, removing from his experiments disturbing variables that upset the equations. If something did not fit into the experiment, it was considered noise. The source of the noise was the chaos in the Universe. Humankind's purpose was to transform that chaos into order under the philosophy that emerged from Newtonian discoveries.

An example of how "chaos" was removed from experimental situations is the famous "three body problem." Newton's model of the solar system was based on simple calculations of the relationship between each planet and the sun. From those calculations, he and subsequent scientists were able to describe the orbits of each planet. They assumed in their calculations that the gravity of the other planets was overwhelmed by the gravitational pull of the sun, and would not affect the stability of the orbits. Through this assumption, they were able to avoid trying to calculate the effect of a third gravitational body—another planet—on the orbit of any other given planet. Thank goodness. The problem was impossible to solve using calculus, because it involved the relationship of two nonlinear formulas.

It was almost 200 years later that the French mathematician, Henri Poincare developed a way to demonstrate that the influence of gravity from a third planet does, in fact, significantly affect the stability of all three planets over the long term. Poincare's work is one of the milestones in developing the new scientific study of complex systems.

Science is full of other examples where a specialized case was generalized because the technology or theory did not exist to solve a problem. For lack of ability, we make predictions on where an arrow will fall based on the laws of gravity, the speed of the arrow, and its trajectory. Meanwhile, we assume that there will be no sudden burst of wind to misdirect the speeding projectile.

Organizations are currently managed the same way. The crux of modern management and leadership is managing—controlling the impact of—change. This means limiting the influence of exterior noise on the workings of organizational systems to ensure that predicted outcomes are achieved. The crux of modern management is to eliminate chaos from the system through control, just as the scientist controls his/her experiment to achieve his/her experimental goals.

The advent of high-speed computers along with concurrent development of new theories of chaos and complex systems has enabled scientists to incorporate much more experimental noise into their equations than was previously believed possible. The discoveries are making such things as genetic engineering and artificial life simulations on computers possible. The results of this process are often quite different from what happens in the controlled conditions of traditional experiments. The result, as you will see throughout this book, is the discovery that some things work differently in reality than previously believed.

Since the older science served as the basis for contemporary management, it behooves us to integrate these new findings into the model. Applying new discoveries about organization exposes the possibility that there may be an inherently more effective mode of organization. It is this new model of organization and its application to organizational systems that will be the subject of this book.

The Quest for Fitness is constructed as an exploration into the science of organization. Many business books offer immediate gratification. Based on the old three-step communication model ("tell them what you are going to tell them…), they give away the core right at the beginning. I've never liked these books. I read the first three chapters and then I'm finished. I like a mystery that forces me to read to the last chapter. I hope you feel that way about this book. Only when each page has something new will you feel that you are receiving the most for your investment.

The book is built around six major components. Chapters one and two create a general model for the study of organizations through an exploration of the latest scientific research. Chapters three and four apply the model to problems of strategic analysis and planning, leading to defining a new approach called *holsight*. Chapters five and six describe a new theory of change and the role that chaos and diversity plays in the change process. Chapter seven applies the change process to a model of continuous adaptation, suggesting a way to move organizations from focused strategies to long term survival. The book concludes with a discussion of the new role of leadership that emerges in long-lived organizations.

A number of other books have recently been written about organizations and the "new science." While the reader will find some similarities between this book and its peers, there is a major distinction. Most other popular authors, whether Peters, Wheatley, or others working on organizational theory, or Davies, Capra and others in the sciences include classical quantum mechanics as a part of the new science. This book aligns itself with the most recent works of Prigogine, Gell-Mann, and others working in the field of quantum chaos, who recognize classical quantum mechanics as part of the "old" Newtonian-based science. This new breed is using complex systems theories to resolve the paradoxes that developed in the classical approach. Such paradoxes as the famous Schroedinger's Cat experiment, which led to a philosophy of an observer-dependent reality, have led some management theorists far astray from rationality. The resolutions now emerging in quantum chaos provides a much more realistic—rational—picture of the nature of our interactions.

Exploration is the fundamental metaphor of this book. Exploration will also become the metaphor of leadership, itself, as the thesis of this book develops. Just as we can think of learning as gaining new understanding, we can think of it as hiking through a jagged landscape, searching for the highest peak. While walking, the exploration of others affects the landscape, interacting with our own search. The search becomes ongoing as a quest for fitness and survival.

This, too, defines the process of scientific inquiry. From the alchemy of the dark ages to the alchemy of artificial intelligence, science seeks ways to improve humankind's relationship to the changing environment. *The Quest for Fitness* will investigate how organizations create their own paths in this ever-changing landscape.

The reader will find at the core of this book my extraordinary experience of over 10 years as the founder and leader of *The Chaos Network*. The Network served as the international focal point of academic and business research in applying complex systems applications to organizations from

1988—1998. During that time, the Network published a quarterly scholarly newsletter, sponsored 5 international conferences, and produced 5 Conference Proceedings along with video and audiotapes.

Internationally recognized scientists such as Nobel Laureates Murray Gell-Mann and Ilya Prigogine, and economist Brian Arthur, made significant contributions to Network members as speakers at the annual conferences. Other key scientists such Alfred Hubler who directs the Center for Complex Systems Research at the University of Illinois, Norman Packard, Gottfried Mayer-Kress, and Richard Morley provided me with personal direction as well as providing access to their work to Network members. And The MetaNetwork (www.tmn.com) provided our members with one of the first on-line interactive discussion communities ever, so that the collaboration could continue on a daily basis.

The results, Network participants such as Ralph Stacey, Jeffrey Goldstein, Stephen Guastello, Brenda Zimmerman, and Glenda Eoyang all published books that were strongly influenced by their co-mingling in the Network. Others such as Kevin Dooley have taken key leadership roles furthering the academic research in this emerging area. Business representatives such as Bill Fulkerson at Deere & Company have achieved national recognition for their contributions to their companies, inspired to some extent by participation in the Network.

Considerable recognition is also due to Lisa Marshall who served as my partner in chaos and motivator through most of the early Network years, to then transcend my work as she co-authored her own book and was named nationally as Trainer of the Year. Additional recognition is due to Dr. Peter Sorensen, Director of the Management and Organizational Behavior Program at Benedictine University. Dr. Sorensen has provided me with support and an academic home for my work without flinching at some of the radical concepts that have flowed through the work over the years.

To all of these pioneering explorers and over 500 other unnamed members of the Network, I offer my deep and humble gratitude.

Accordingly, I ask that the reader consider this book as not just the musings of one author, but the edification of the contributions of all of these explorers. For I am certain that as you read the forthcoming words you will recognize that this book has emerged from our combined work as deliciously as the broth that brews in the old Yiddish story *Stone Soup*, which clearly foresaw much of the findings of chaos theory.

Mark Michaels
June, 2000
Urbana, Illinois, USA

Chapter 1

Science as a Lens of Understanding

Creation Story 1

In the beginning, the world was created through the division of the serpent, Chaos, into land and sky. Within the sky was created the layers of heaven for the birds, the sun and moon, the stars, the angels, upward in that order. Below the earth was created the nether world, the land of darkness. The sun, stars, and moon were placed in the heavens, and were commanded to circle the earth, creating and dividing time into day and night. Upon the earth was placed all forms of beings that would ever exist. Finally, human kind was placed on the earth and charged with having dominion over all of the earth.

Life on earth proved to be harsh. Humans proved to be imperfect. Learning of good and evil, they were banished from the perfected garden. Because Chaos still dwelled outside of the garden and within the earth, the Gates of Paradise moved further and further from view. Redemption became our purpose. We strove to return to Paradise, to the Garden, to timeless immortality.

Creation Story 2

There is no beginning, there is no end, only an endless cycle of creation, destruction, and re-creation. Each re-creation forms from the same materials within the egg-like dimension of the never-dying universe. The land, animal species, and humans are all created together each time, They all disappear at the moment of destruction.

Within this major cycle exists the circle of life. Day and night, birth and death, planting and harvesting, summer's warmth and winter's cold, key cycles within the larger universal cycle. All act together as though parts of a clock.

Humans seek to escape the illusion of time, the world of endless renewal, as the Greek god Sisyphus pleaded to be relieved of his task rolling the stone wheel back up the mountain. Humans seek release through kind and meditative acts. With each rebirth and each meditative emancipation, believers hope to come one step closer to the point of release.

Creation Story 3

About 12 billion years ago, give or take 3 billion years, there was a big bang. Or maybe it was the beginning of a new bubble expanding, emerging from an older universe. Perhaps it was just another instability randomly erupting in one of an infinite number of quantum fields. It may not be possible to actually know how it all got started.

Since shortly after that beginning, atoms have been bouncing against each other like billiard balls on a pool table. The interaction is disorderly, unpredictable, and unrepeatable.

It seems a miracle that order has developed from these random interactions. There was eventually enough bouncing around that some atoms began to stick together, forming larger atoms and molecules. Interactions grew into development of stars and planets, then organic molecules, and eventually plants, animals, and human beings. Each of these developments represents a new level of organization. Yet at the base, quantum particles which are the ghosts of our beginnings, continue to act in weird, chaotic ways.

The Universe continues to create itself to this day. It is an engine of continual expansion and constant change. The new is always being created, although by human time it can take a long time to happen. Expansion has resulted in increased complexity. At the start, when the Universe was simple, organization was simple, just a system of four interacting forces. As the universe evolved, organization developed both as an adaptation to and the cause of this complexification.

Since close to the beginning there has been purpose to organization. Organization redirects entropy—warding off dissipation into a cold death. Organization saves the Universe from the image that every child sees when s/he tosses a handful of ping pong balls into a bucket. They bounce around a while and then fall still at the bottom of the bucket.

In this dance of energy, first, inorganic substances acquired the ability to organize. Through their interaction, energy was conserved, redirected, and even created from some of the matter. The Universe became robust. Nevertheless, the unrelenting expansion of the universe

made the struggle more complex. Newer responses, includ-
ing organic molecules and life, itself, emerged as part of the
continual creation. Humans developed as one of the more
adaptive systems within this ever-changing universe.

The Science of Creation and the Purpose of Organization

Science is humankind's method for describing our environment. The scientific method has existed for at least four thousand years. What has changed is the capacity of the tools of science. The Babylonian creation story that represents the first example was written by the astronomers, physicians, and other scientists of their time with very primitive tools for observation. The court astrologers, philosophers, and alchemists served as the advisors to the earlier leaders, providing the most advanced technologies available.

There are numerous creation stories. Each culture has its own story about how the Universe, world, and their culture came to be. The stories came from a culture's search to understand its existence. The answers would be found in the relationship between a culture, its tools, and its environment.

Anthropologists add that creation stories are myths that also represent a culture's worldview. It defines one's purpose on earth. That makes sense. If you know how the earth was created, it tells you something about why you exist. If you think that your responsibility to the world is to dominate it as you rebuild paradise, as commanded in the first creation story, then you will act differently than others who feel that they are just sojourners on a cyclical path.

When the many disparate creation stories are compared, they appear to fall into three categories, as summarized above. The first two stories are composites, representing the stories most commonly found in a number of religions today. But precedent for the third story can also be found in religious mythology. In fact, all three stories are often found in the same religion at different points in time. One or another then falls in and out of favor throughout the centuries. [2]

The first composite creation story developed in landed cultures such as Babylon. These are the cultures responsible for creation of the first city-states, which valued centralization of power, and application of that power to win wars and build massive architectural structures. Such achievements are related to the values and behaviors found between the lines of that creation story.

Cultures tied to the first creation story originally experienced the broader Universe as unchanging over time. The rotation of the stars were set in the heavens at the time of creation, as was the course of the sun and moon. The heavens were, according to Aristotle, an "ather" world, an unchanging constellation in the sky.

What does change in this story is the condition of the earth and of humans who dwell on it. While the Universe was created through the defeat of the serpent Chaos by the forces of order, the world is now degenerating back into the clutches of Chaos. The reason for decline is the failure of humans to fulfill their original mission to tend to the primordial garden. Obstacles are placed across our path in this quest, evil tempts us, and we frequently bend to its demands.

If our responsibility is to dominate the earth, controlling Chaos in order to maintain the creation, then humans organize to halt this decline. We can conquer evil, take control and fix the world to fit our vision of paradise.

---

2 One of the interesting aspects of the creation stories is their use of time. In the first two stories, time is an illusion. But time is an integral part of the third story. Timothy Ferris, in *The Whole Shebang, A state-of-the-universe(s) report* explains how the "Jews of old obstinately refused to dismiss time as an illusion," continuing to explain how the creation story in Genesis "ticks like a clock," and how, by depicting history as a story, the early Christians took a similar attitude.

Sir Isaac Newton's research (along with the works of Kepler and Copernicus), from which he developed the laws of motion, was condemned for identifying that neither earth nor humankind was at the physical center of the Universe. But his theories also served to reinforce this creation story. Our image of the universe as a clock-like mechanical function reinforced the notion of the world as never changing. There could be change within our world, but it was within a never changing structure of the Universe.[3]

The industrial revolution in the West was both a product of and metaphor for this creation story. Industrialists such as J. Paul Getty, Henry Ford, the Rockefellers and others created the railroads, major banks, and modern industry during this time. "Scientific Management" and the creation of the assembly line were appropriate tools helping fulfill these quests. The Industrial Revolution could not have succeeded without the mechanical view of the Universe and the development of Newton's laws of motion.

The second creation story comes from cultures whose environment made them dependent upon the cycles of time. This dependency could have resulted from cycling through a group of hunting sites throughout the year, from developing an agrarian culture with dependence on the seasons, or from the cycles of high and low water along a major river such as the Nile or the Ganges rivers.

Cultures whose thinking is dominated by the second creation story have less of a history of development, in the modern sense. They were more likely to be subjugated by dominating cultures. Yet within this worldview, subjugation does not matter. Maybe patience is misunderstood as wisdom because those with a cyclical worldview demonstrate

---

3 It is legitimate to state that the notion of a clockwork universe also reinforced the cyclical worldview, since the clock does represent the cycles of time. However, it may be more appropriate to state that Newton's thesis actually merged the two world views into one of an internally dynamic, yet ultimately never changing universe.

patience resulting from their trust in the cycles of time. What happens on a daily basis is of little importance to those with a cyclical worldview, so long as the cycle is not expected to change.

The cyclical worldview has been emerging over the past 30 years as an acceptable world view for Westerners. Two popular songs, "From a Distance" sung by Bette Midler, and "Circle of Life" sung by Elton John (from the Disney movie *The Lion King*) both express the cyclical worldview. Current interest in the wisdom of the American Indian is presented with an eye on the cycles of life. The worldview is seen in our actions towards recycling and in our environmental activities to maintain ecological niches as understood from the popular notion of sustainable environments. The latter is built from a simple systems model relating the predators and prey, a model that will be explored at some length in later chapters. In all of these instances, the cycle stems from a natural world view related to the earth's recent history.

Life under the first creation story requires decisiveness, creativity, and domination, overpowering obstacles to create the world in one's image. Balance replaces domination in the second story. Fitting within the system is key, not overtaking the system. This leader does not seek to rock the boat. We strive to keep it on course, to keep on an even keel.

A third world view is now emerging. It comes from the same source as the first two worldviews, from the science of our time. By science I mean the process by which we observe our surroundings, create inferences about the functioning of our surroundings that are confirmed by the observation of others, and use such knowledge to effectively adapt to changes in our environment.

This book looks to science as it is developing today to learn about the new world view, and apply it to organizations. It is intended as a guide to modern leaders who realize that leadership is built on the foundation of an accurate worldview, enabling us to understand our role in the universe.

Continuation of the New Creation Story

Remarkably, from the simplicity of creation emerged organization, first in the inorganic world, and then the living world. Atoms formed into matter. At least on Earth, a biosphere became organized, which we experience as a collection of interacting ecosystems—forests, lakes, and seas teeming with wildlife. Organization eventually emerged into social relationships. Trees grow to different heights to improve their access to light and earth minerals, birds flock, bees and ants do their chores in service to their queen. Self-organization generated new modes of survival.

A central function in this story is self-organization. Self-organization can be found within regular statistical processes. Systems come together because they are the most likely ones to come together. As Kauffman observed, we get order for free.[4]

How does self-organization work? While it will be explained in detail in Chapter 6, a example can be described here. Consider rolling dice. When rolling 1 die, there is a one in six chance of rolling any one of the six sides. As a result, if, over time, we roll a lot more sixes than any other number, we will rightfully suspect that the die is loaded. But when rolling two dice, the whole structure of the roll changes. We do not have a one in twelve chance to roll any possible number. There is only one way to get a two or a twelve. There are five ways to roll a six. So if, in the long run, we **do not** roll more sixes than twos or twelves, we would become suspicious of the dice.

The same is true of the physical world. Those combinations of atoms, molecules, etc., which could connect more frequently because of their availability, did connect more frequently.

The force of the big bang, or the energy associated with the expansion of the new bubble pushes the primordial substances together to

---

4 Kauffman, Stuart. *At Home in the Universe.*

form the matter which becomes our Universe. The rules of probability moved the Universe from a simple system relating four basic forces to a series of highly complex interactions. As the complexity increased, systems self-organized in response to the increased complexity. Eventually, a process of co-evolution developed.

Human organizations are artifacts of the Universe's beginnings. Organization is how we come together to achieve efficient use of our resources in response to our complex environment. We search for and develop efficient resource use to enable us to survive. For humans, as for other species, organization is a natural tool for survival.

This emerging creation story establishes a totally different purpose for humankind. The story takes humankind off of its pedestal of domination and out of the cycle of fate. Instead of being the superior product of creation, we become part of creation. Instead of being responsible for either continuing the creation or stewarding its results, we have new responsibilities.

As a part of a continuing creation, we find ourselves struggling to survive in response to changes around us. At the same time, our struggles cause more change around us, new vistas to explore, to understand, to become adapted to. We create and respond to creation. There is always something new before us. It is as if humankind is on a constant journey to new worlds. Only those new worlds exist within our midst.

Success is Not Growth

In the worldview of domination, success, achieving one's purpose, is defined in terms of control. Domination means being able to bend the world to fit one's requirements. Control of resources and beating the competition are the gauges of success.

For instance, a dominating culture will assess the extent to which the earth supports its needs for an ever-improved quality of life. The forest and jungle are wild and chaotic, they have not yet come under control. The society turns these areas into cities, parks, cultured fields, or nature preserves, transforming chaos into order.

In business, domination is measured by control of resources and the market place. A high return on one's investment demonstrates control over one's resources. Vertical acquisitions and mergers achieve control of resources. This allows the leader to control the process from basic resource acquisition to distribution and sales. The economics of such activity leads to centralization to strengthen control and achieve economy of scale.

Control in the face of competition requires continuous growth. Investors love companies when they demonstrate that they can continue to increase their revenues by five or ten percent per year, year in and year out. If, by chance, there is a year without growth, investors bail out quickly, like rats leaving a sinking ship.

For dominating organizations, every action is a competition, a war. Businesses fight for market share—to be the first to be on top when the market completes its growth phase. While vertical integration allows for control of resources, horizontal integration through mergers and acquisitions enables the company to buy market share. Strategies such as control of patents and extensive, controlled distribution systems are used to acquire market share, furthering the chances for control. The hope is that once the market size tops out, (because all markets are finite in size), the Conqueror's organization will still be standing.

I am always amazed at how many corporate vision or mission statements envision the company as being the "dominant market leader" and then defining the strategy by which this will be achieved. Microsoft's mission exemplifies the urge to dominate. It reads:

"At Microsoft, our long-held vision of a computer on every desk and in every home continues to be at the core of everything we do. We are committed to the belief that software is the tool that empowers people both at work and at

home. Since our company was founded in 1975, our charter has been to deliver on this vision of the power of personal computing.

"As the world's leading software provider, we strive to continually produce innovative products that meet the evolving needs of our customers. Our extensive commitment to research and development is coupled with dedicated responsiveness to customer feedback. This allows us to explore future technological advancements, while assuring that our customers today receive the highest quality software products."[5]

It is also amazing how most companies never achieve this goal, many even claim it but do not really strive for it. That is because there can only be one number one at the head of a list.

For years, Ford has demonstrated that a company can be an excellent investment even when it is not the largest company overall. Subaru and Honda are two companies that recognize that they have little chance of dominating their markets, but remain solid investments.

IBM is to a market like a bull is to a china shop, constantly upsetting the status quo. While it is one of the largest companies overall, it is now rare for the IBM to be the dominant player in any given market for long. For instance, personal computer clones continue to have a much larger market share of the personal computer market, yet IBM continues to be a critical player on the field.

At the same time, growth-dominated companies such as Sears, General Motors, and Chrysler, tend to become like dinosaurs. They move beyond a point of adaptability, becoming maladapted to their environments. They last a while under such conditions, but when the

---

5 From www.microsoft.com web site

market is shocked, such as when the airline industry was deregulated, they fall hard, as was the case for Pan American Airways.

It is not as easy to define what success means for organizations conforming to a cyclical worldview. These companies are more sensitive to the impact that they have on their environment. So it may be appropriate to understand their definition of success as "fitting in," and their motto as "do no harm."

Contrast the mission statement for Ben & Jerry's Ice Cream against the one above for Microsoft:

> "Product: To make, distribute and sell the finest quality all natural ice cream and related products in a wide variety of innovative flavors made from Vermont dairy products.
>
> Economic: To operate the Company on a sound financial basis of profitable growth, increasing value for our shareholders, and creating career opportunities and financial rewards for our employees.
>
> Social: To operate the Company in a way that actively recognizes the central role that business plays in the structure of society by initiating innovative ways to improve the quality of life of a broad community—local, national, and international.
>
> Underlying the mission of Ben & Jerry's is the determination to seek new and creative ways of addressing all three parts, while holding a deep respect for the individuals, inside & outside the company, and for the communities of which they are a part[6].

Both mission statements talk about growth. Microsoft's is virtually unlimited, seeing a computer on every desk and in every home—world

---

6 From www.benjerry.com

domination. Ben & Jerry's growth is controlled by its desire to fit into its environment, and to fulfill its social responsibilities. Given a choice of growth or having a negative impact on the environment, Ben & Jerry's has a history of protecting the environment. In fact, the company has made specific decisions, such as its use of milk from cows who have not been fed with Recombinant Bovine Growth Hormone, its recycling efforts, and its policy to contribute to various charities, which tend to limit the potential for domination.

What is interesting is to compare the growth in stock price of the two companies. Microsoft's stock has skyrocketed over the past 10 years. The chart is consistent with that of a product life cycle or organizational life cycle chart for an organization tied to a fast growing market. (Figure 1-1). At the time of this writing, it appears as though the stock may be reaching the maturation point—the point where it tops out and begins to decline. While the industry generally feels that this is impossible, if we remember that Microsoft's success is grounded in the technology of a personal computer operating system, then the possibility of decline becomes visible. The issue, will Microsoft be able and allowed to adapt when a new technology—a new operating system -overshadows the basic DOS/Windows operating system. An upstart, Sun System's JAVA, is waiting in the wings to take over. JAVA reduces the need for an operating system, while breaking down the wall between individual computers and the World Wide Web.[7]

---

7 Microsoft has acted decisively to adapt to the market's change. When Netscape emerged as the leading program for web browsing, Microsoft quickly established relationships that led to developing a competitive product, and then used its extensive distribution system to effectively challenge Netscape. Microsoft is now developing its own version of JAVA in response to this unsettling development. However, the company appears to be facing a brick wall of social control in its attempt to survive by defining and controlling the new market. Microsoft's means of domination are being challenged by the Federal and state governments. The issue is not whether Microsoft has a right to dominate the emerging Internet-based computer structure, but whether it has a right to leverage its domination of the current structure to achieve this goal. It is a classical conflict between a domination worldview and a cyclical world view in which ownership is secondary to relationship.

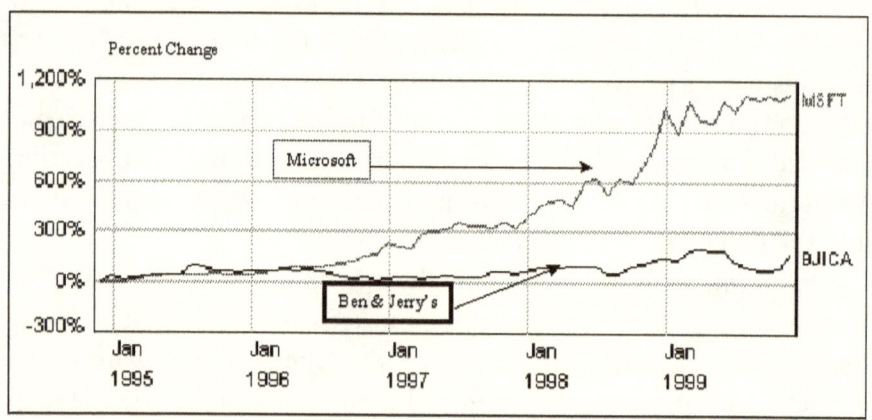

Figure 1-1: 5 Year Stock Comparison (as of 12/7/99)

In contrast, Ben & Jerry's stock rose quickly for its first 3 years, consistent with an Initial Price Offering of stock, then dropped to a point around which it has consistently cycled for the past four years. A comparison of 1997 stock prices, when the stock market continued to rise fairly consistently except for the October crash, shows Microsoft experiencing a comparative rise during the first half, following which it began its first consistent slide in its history. In the mean time, Ben and Jerry's stock fluctuated consistently between its high and low. Yet no one suggests that Ben & Jerry's is moving towards closure.

Can it really be said the Ben & Jerry's is not successful because it lacks growth?

Change as a Measure of Success

In the first two creation stories, change is the exception. The human's role regarding change is corrective, to swing the system back in line with the plan.

The three key lessons of the new creation story are:

1)   We live in a world of continuous change;
2)   We help generate that change; and
3)   We cannot control the change.

In 1988, when chaos/complex systems theory first became popular, management theorists such as Peter Vaill and Alvin Toeffler[8] began offering new strategies addressing the problem of continuous change. However, they stuck with the linear concept of improving the management functions of planning and control. Seminars on Managing Change became the order of the day. Managing change meant controlling change. The strategy was to make a plan, (have a vision or goal), follow that plan, and to find ways to reduce the impact of outside interference as much as possible so you would stay as much on the predetermined course as possible. What was not understood was that continuous change exists within organizations as well as in their external environments.

In 1988, using chaos theory as my guide, I developed a participatory exercise called *The Chaos Exercise* to demonstrate the problem. The exercise starts with three organizational levels representing production, management, and executives. Most of the action is at the bottom, on the production line. That team tosses balls in a pattern to symbolize the movement of materials through the production line. As the team works,

---

8 Vaill describes how organizations operate in an environment of constant change with his description of "permanent white water" in *Managing as a performing Art*. Alvin Toeffler noted how change was becoming a common day reality for organizations in *The Third Wave*

the facilitator intervenes with everyday occurrences: pulling people out for meetings, phone calls, or vacation; simulating a strike; making a tornado go through the plant, etc. Production is tracked and always proves to be irregular because of these unplanned events.

After about ten minutes, the teams are invited to put their heads together and plan ways in which they can improve their work. Over the years, teams have developed numerous strategies to try to minimize the chaos coming from both within and outside the organizations. (My favorite was their request to fire the facilitator!) Internal generators of chaos, such as different skill levels and team confusion, are even addressed by some. The teams are then given another ten minutes to try out their plan, with the facilitator continuing to insert random events into the process.

Comparing the results of the first and second part of *The Chaos Exercise* exposes the fallacy of this strategy. When the output from the second half was compared with the output from the first, the randomness of the output continued. Often, but not always, the total output actually decreased. All attempts to reduce the effect of chaos on the organizational system backfired. Participants realized that internally as well as externally driven change is continuous, regardless of their efforts.

There was another, stronger lesson in *The Chaos Exercise.* Participants also realized that change is not controllable! Because it is uncontrollable, change is also unpredictable.[9]

In practice, change is generated by forces outside the organization and as a result of our own actions. As an organization changes, for instance, as it invents a new product, the product's development and production impacts what is going on around the organization.

---

9 Was this real chaos in terms of the scientific study of the phenomena? Stephen Guastello conducted the exercise a number of times. He then conducted a mathematical review of the results. The answer was, yes, this is exactly what the mathematicians were talking about! See Guastello, Stephen, *Chaos, Catastrophe, and Human Affairs*

An example of this relationship can be found by studying the impact of human behavior on the environment. This issue became important during the 1970s when environmentalism came into vogue. But the environmentalists' picture represented only part of the story—society's impact on the environment. The environmentalists established the goal of controlling change that affects the environment, which they try to implement through heavy regulation of new industry and technology. As we will see in the discussion of controlling chaos in Chapter 5, such control is no more possible than controlling change in organizations.[10] More specifically, environmentalists failed to consider the entire, co-evolutionary loop. Once the environment changes, we change our processes to adapt to the changes, since we will never be able to stop the change.

In 1980, the economist Julian Simon wagered a bet against Paul Ehrlich, a doomsday environmentalist. At the time, environmentalists were complaining that runaway population growth and the changes that we made through the development of our industrial society in response to that growth were going to deplete the basic resources of the world. This, environmentalists claimed, was placing us in danger of early annihilation. Simon bet that resources were not becoming depleted and that the claims were not supportable.

To measure change for the bet, Ehrlich picked 5 metals in heavy use at the time: chromium, copper, nickel, tin, and tungsten. Ehrlich and his colleagues determined that these resources were in danger of depletion. Simon proposed that the depletion of resources could be tracked by using a measure of scarcity, the price of the resource. If the price went up, the resource would be considered scarcer. The bet was to last 10 years.

---

10 Our lack of ability to control nature or its effects on us was first made clear to me in 1970 by my professor of geological science at Penn State University, Gerald Lattman. Dr. Lattman described the Army Corp of Engineers' continued attempts to control the Mississippi, and how the mighty river always wins out.

In 1990, Ehrlich presented Simon with a check for $576.07. The price of all five metals had declined, and some, like tin, had declined considerably. The resources were not becoming depleted.[11]

What had happened? Substitutions had been invented in the interim for some of the resources. These substitutions led to a decrease in demand for the resources, lowering their value, and their use.

These examples demonstrate that success is not dependent on the ability to manage change. The opposite may be true. Controlling change may actually reduce one's chances for success. This is a central focus of thesis of this book.

Fitness as a Measure of Success

The birth of the new creation story can be traced back to Charles Darwin. [12] Darwin's proposal that species adapted to their local environment put an end to the notion of an unchanging universe. (This was soon followed by Einstein's Theory of Relativity and research in astronomy, which demonstrated that galaxies and stars are moving relative to each other. This put the final nail on the coffin of the Ptolemic Universe model, which had existed for almost 2000 years.)

The image that we have of Darwin's theory is that of survival of the fittest. We envision two species fighting it out for the same

---

11 "The Doomslayer" by Ed Regis, from *Wired Magazine,* Vol. 5(2). Simon consistently faced opposition to his studies from environmentalists, acting as stewards in their attempts to control the natural process of change to maintain previously established conditions. Yet Simon had a strong track record of being correct in his predictions, as opposed to the continual inaccuracy of the doomsday environmentalists. While preparing this section of the book, I had the opportunity to begin an e-mail dialogue with Simon, only to learn shortly thereafter of his untimely death. Chaos has given us all a great loss of rationality and sanity.

12 See Chapter 2 on the history and sources of complexity theory

resources until one of them overpowers the other and takes control of the environment.

But this was not what Darwin had in mind. Individual animals and plants did not physically compete in Darwin's evolving universe. The competition was mostly within specie groups, the process of adaptation through mutation and selection. If a mutation helped the species survive, it was carried on to future generations. If it hurt survival efforts, the mutation was discontinued. If the environment changed, a new mutation might prove more adaptable, and would be selected for replication over time.

Others, following Darwin's theory, added the theme of competition within ecological niches. Competition between species became a metaphor for competition between peoples. The most fit would survive. Social Darwinism lead to other misconceptions and excesses, eventually leading up to the horror of the Holocaust in World War II. The result gave the notion of fitness a bad name.

Contemporary biologists have rejected Social Darwinism, but not the notion of fitness. Biologists, such as Stephen Jay Gould, Stuart Kauffman, and Richard Dawkins. have demonstrated that evolution is a process of mutation that enables adaptability. From adaptation emerges fitness.

These contemporary biologists have added another component to fitness. Fitness is now seen as an ever-changing condition, in line with the ever changing nature of the Universe. At any given time in any given ecological niche there exists both fit and unfit specimens. Darwinian fitness pictured a process where first the environment changed, then a few new specie members mutated to an acceptable adaptation, and his/her gene was carried through into the future by future generations replicating the gene and its resulting biological change.

The contemporary biologist sees diversity as consistent at all times within any species hoping to survive. While there may be a dominant form at a given time, other forms co-exist. When conditions change favoring one of the minorities of the group, the minority will prosper to maintain the species in some form.[13]

Two examples make this point. First, consider the problems that are now emerging concerning the control of staphylococcus bacteria. This is a bacteria which we thought we had eliminated with modern anti-biotics. What has been learned is that as the dominant strains were significantly reduced in numbers with the anti-biotics, other strains, which could survive, found that they were no longer competing for resources. Therefore, the resistant strains could now prosper.

A more surprising example concerns the extinction of dinosaurs. They all died off 3 million years ago—right? Wrong. Research now shows that they have survived and live among us. No, we are not talking about the Lock Ness Monster or the crocodile (which is a reptile that is an ancestor of the dinosaur). The descendants of dinosaurs are the beautiful birds that fly overhead! When the earth cooled as a result of the dust from a meteor impact in Mexico (current theory) causing dinosaurs to die out, one form, which could easily migrate to safer areas lived on. These are the ancestors of the birds of today.

These examples demonstrate a new understanding of fitness. Fitness is not only a measure of status at one point in time. It is also a measure of adaptability. In the new creativity story, success is defined as fitness. But because of continuous change, included in the definition of fitness is the ability to adapt. Adaptability it turns out, is a function of diversity.

In the new creation story, life is a passage through the wilderness of time. While on that passage, we constantly experience the unexpected. To survive requires the resources that enable quick adaptation to the unexpected. To stand still is to die.

---

13 See Gould, Stephen J, *Wonderful Life: The Burgess Shale and the Nature of History* and Lewin, Roger, *Complexity, Life on the Edge of Chaos*

Chapter 2

Applying 7 New Scientific Principles

Dupont Corporation had a production problem. They were making a thin film material. The process involved running a sharp knife over a jelly like substance to create a uniform width and smooth coat. When the knife moved at slow speeds everything worked smoothly. But there was a limit that could not be broken—a production speed above which ripples would develop in the film. There was no traditional way to overcome this barrier.

Modern, complex organizations appear to be reaching a similar barrier. The push for increased capacity and productivity, just in time inventory, short run manufacturing strategies, high speed information acquisition, increased product lines, diversification, and personalized service are working together to push organizations up against an invisible barrier. It is a barrier we have always feared—*the edge of chaos.*

Eventually, this book will convince you that the *edge of chaos* is not a barrier. While it may feel like Alice's Wonderland, it really is the place for adaptation and growth. It appears to be a barrier because traditional management theory is built on the scientific principles of linear dynamics developed by Sir Isaac Newton. Linear dynamics treats chaos as noise. The power of chaotic processes is hidden to the linear investigator.

There is no such thing as complexity in Newtonian science. Complexity, to a Newtonian, is just the accumulation of a series of simple systems into a larger, simple system. You may remember being taught in high school physics that all machines were built from seven basic machines—the pulley, the screw, the lever, the wedge, the wheel, the axle, and the inclined plain. Understanding and fixing a machine was a matter of breaking it down into these basic machines. The concept that larger systems are understood by understanding the dynamics of their constituent parts is called reductionism.

By definition, linear construction allows for quantitative prediction of future events from an understanding of past and current conditions of the system. The future is a straight, "logical" line that stretches from where we were to where we are going.

Traditional strategic planning is built on a linear approach to management. The following example demonstrates the linearity of and problems with the traditional approach.

Company A establishes a mission to increase its stock value during the next five years by maintaining market leadership in the automobile (or any other) industry. A plan is developed to achieve the mission with long and short-term steps called goals and objectives. The plan is based on a formula that works something like this:

- *Based on market growth projections, Company A anticipates the need to build a total of Y automobiles in the next 5 years.*
- *Each car costs M dollars to build and N dollars to market.*
- *Stockholders demand $Q profit during each year to support a rising stock price.*
- *Therefore, revenues will need to be $Z in the next 5 years to achieve the mission of maintaining a rising stock price each year.*
- *To determine the value of $Z, we use a mathematical formula:*
- *$Z=Y(M +N +Q)$*
- *(Revenues needed will equal the number of automobiles to be built times the sum of the marketing costs, manufacturing costs, and profits.)*

The above formula is very straightforward, linear, and constitutes the type of math every cost accountant uses. However, each item is built from at least one secondary formula. The secondary formulas might include a market growth formula, unit costs formula, and a formula to project inflation rates.

As plan and implementation proceeds, it may become necessary to change the information in one of the formulas. Based on traditional theory, an assumption is made that any change, small or large, in any one of the secondary formulas will result in only an equivalent change in outcomes of the larger formula. If the inflation rate is higher than planned, or the cost per car goes down, we believe that we can change other parts of the formula to achieve the revenues for which we originally planned.

Unfortunately, these assumptions have proven to be false. Some of the secondary formulas are nonlinear. A key dynamic of nonlinear formulas is that they demonstrate a potential for multiple solutions. The end result will likely be something other than predicted.

Consider, for instance, one equation that can help model market growth. This is a formula that shows the relationship between market size and number of competitors. The product life cycle demonstrates that when the market for a product reaches the growth phase, competitors jump in, resulting in lower prices. During the maturity phase, consolidation takes place through merger, acquisition, and bankruptcy. With the decrease in competitors, increased demand raises prices again. Decline sets in as market size decreases due to higher prices and the creation of alternative, less expensive replacement products.

Such changes appear to follow a very specific nonlinear formula called the *logistics equation*:

$$X_{n+1} = KX_n(1 - X_n)$$

In this formula, X represents the number of competitors in the industry. K is a constant that represents the difference between supply and demand. The formula is iterative over time, which means that each solution (X_{n+1}) is built from the last solution to the formula (X_n).

Now, if the difference between supply and demand is low, it turns out that this is a very predictable formula. Regardless of the number of competitors in the industry at the start, the number will eventually stabilize. But as the supply/demand ratio increases, the number of competitors oscillates. As that ratio exceeds 3.56, we see an explosion of possible solutions to the formula, making it impossible to predict the number of competitors in the market based on the initial market starting conditions. This explosion is demonstrated in a graph of the equation in Figure 2-1

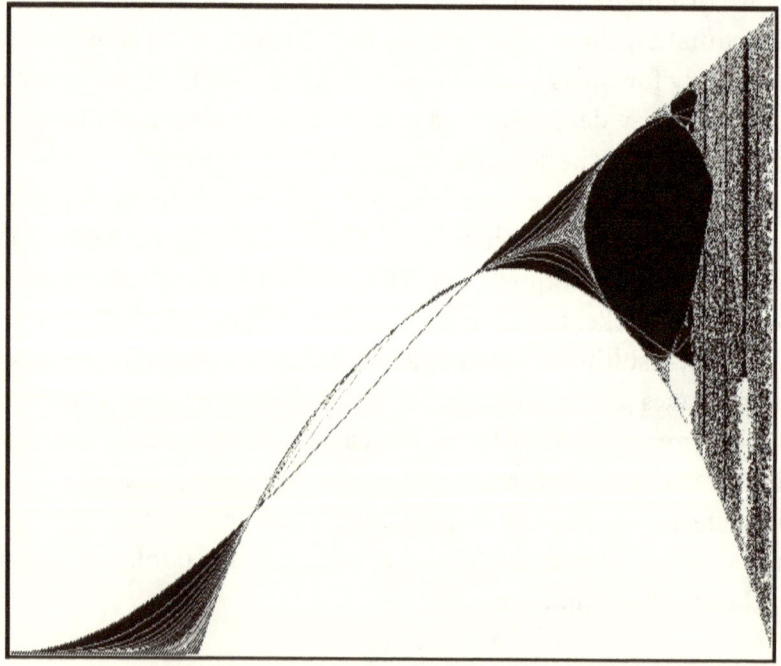

Figure 2-1: The Logistics Map

Such an unstable market model cannot be easily integrated into a predictable strategic plan, yet that's what we consistently try to do.

The number 3.56 in the above formula represents the *edge of chaos*. Once over the edge, using the formula for simple predictions becomes impossible. Any small change in the plan can develop into wildly unexpected outcomes. This does not fit into how we currently understand our organizations.

Quality Management, reengineering, and other popular business strategies have each been called a "paradigm shift." But the scientific revolution building from complex systems theory, like its predecessor that emerged from Newton's work, is a much more fundamental shift in our world view than now implied by the word paradigm. How fundamental is the shift? The great astrophysicist, Stephen Hawking, looking at science from Newton's chair at Oxford, has suggested that we are at the end of science—at least in it's ability to achieve its mission of explaining how the universe functions. However, Nobel Laureate Ilya Prigogine, looking at developments in the new science, countered, "In contrast, we believe that we are actually at the beginning of a new scientific era. We are observing the birth of a science that is no longer limited to idealized and simplified situations but reflects the complexity of the real world, a science that views us and our creativity as part of a fundamental trend present in nature"[14]

Newton's universal schema, calculus and the laws of gravity, served as the foundation for the industrial revolution. The giant steam turbine machines of the 19th century that were demonstrated at world fairs in

---

14 Prigogine, Ilya. *The End of Certainty: Time, Chaos and the New Laws of Nature.* p. 7. More specifically, Hawking cautiously predicted in a lecture at Cambridge University in 1980 that we may reach the goal of theoretical physics, to have a "complete, consistent, and unified theory of the physical interactions which would describe all possible observations," by around the end of the century. Boslough, John, *Stephen Hawking's Universe*, "Appendix: Is the End in Sight for Theoretical Physics? An Inaugural Lecture." I first heard Prigogine make this same comparison in a speech at the University of Illinois, April 17, 1992

places like Philadelphia, and Chicago, are towering monuments to linearity. The modern bureaucratic organization and assembly line are the ultimate social creations of the science.

The film ripples that develop from a fast moving knife at Dupont is just one more example of this seemingly unbreakable barrier, the edge of chaos. But Dupont found a way to go beyond this edge. Its solution was to make the knife jagged at the higher speeds. The new style blade offset the instabilities that developed when the film moved at higher speeds.[15]

Research at Dupont and places like the Santa Fe Institute are making it possible to go beyond the edge of chaos. What held us back previously? The answer, while the earliest developments in the science of complexity happened in the late 19th century, the field could not mature until the advent of high speed computers and a more open social environment. Now, the ability to transcend the barrier is showing us surprising differences between how we thought we could do things and how we actually can.

To make our organizations effective on the other side of the edge of chaos will require even more radical approaches to how we do things than found in Dupont's solution.

Starting With A Systems Perspective

The journey to the edge of chaos starts with an understanding of systems. Surprisingly, many managers fail to understand the nature of systems.

---

15 The same concept is being applied to a number of other objects that collide with the edge of chaos, ranging from golf balls to airplane wings.

A system is, very simply, an organization of related parts that, when acting together, behaves in some identifiable manner. Examples of such systems include the ecological system, a manufacturing system, and the endocrine system. Three rocks, sitting side by side without touching are generally considered not to be a system because their interaction (based on gravitational pull) is negligible. But pile the three rocks on top of each other and they become a system (unstable at first, moving into a stable behavior), because they interact with each other.

Organizations develop and use many systems, including the manufacturing, financial, information, and human resource management systems. In such systems, the *input* may be materials, financial resources, and worker skills. The *process* is the interaction of these resources resulting in some change—or added value—to the customer over the value of the parts when separate. All of the inputs or resources actually change in the process, and the *outcomes* are the changes in these resources.

Traditional systems analysis assesses the changes in the resources: $X and Y worker hours lost by the company coupled with customer gains in C value. These three variables are the system *outputs* or *outcomes*. This analysis is linear, in that it is assumed that one can predict and control the outcomes. The manager only has to know the inputs and understand the functioning of the system, which is done by observing the functioning of smaller system parts. But this strategy fails to work with nonlinear systems.

Systems include one additional function—*feedback*. Feedback in mechanical systems represents the flow of information. In organizational systems, it is usually thought of as the stuff that enables the system to adjust. Traditional management methods use feedback to manipulate system outcomes by changing inputs and processes to achieve the required quality outputs. In the manufacturing example, feedback brings about changes in how much money and worker hours are used, adjusting in how much value is going to the customer. If customer value is to be improved or reduced, that can then supposedly be done by adjusting the inputs and process accordingly.

For instance, if it takes $10,000 plus 40 worker hours to serve 10 customers adequately, and we want to improve the quality of service, we then assume that it will take (maybe) $15,000 plus 40 worker hours. But good leaders know that this kind of thinking actually takes us up against the barrier again. If the formula worked in reality, it would be easy to fix all sorts of problems from the health care crises to the education problems in this country.

There are two types of feedback, balancing and reinforcing. Both types interact in ways which can both amuse and amaze.

Balancing feedback[16] is the type of feedback most common to organizational planning. Balancing feedback maintains a system within pre-specified boundaries. Thermostats linked to heating systems, for instance, are balancing feedback systems because they keep the system operating so that a room stays within pre-set temperature limits. Management by Objectives and other appraisal systems are usually practiced as balancing feedback systems, establishing parameters of behavior and keeping performance within those parameters.

Reinforcing feedback[17] is the iteration of information within the system over time. By iteration, we mean that the output of the system is fed back into the system as the start of its next action. An example is the feedback that develops when a microphone is held up to a connected loud speaker. The system quickly produces a squelch.

---

16 Balancing feedback is traditionally called negative feedback. However, the word "negative" contains too many negative implications including a false assumption that this is bad feedback.

17 Reinforcing feedback is traditionally called positive feedback. However, it, too, contains too many incorrect connotations, including confusion with use of the term in psychology. In his book, The Fifth Discipline Peter Senge uses the term, "snow ball effect" as his alternative.

Budgeting is frequently an iterative process. Revenues from a previous year are fed back into the system as financial targets for the next year, unless there is a major business plan change.

Balancing feedback restricts or dampens change. Reinforcing feedback fosters change. Take, for instance, the relationship between quality and customer expectations. As demonstrated in Figure 2-2, there is an "evolutionary" relationship between the two. As quality improves, it increases the expectations of clients, which then forces quality to again improve, again raising client expectations.

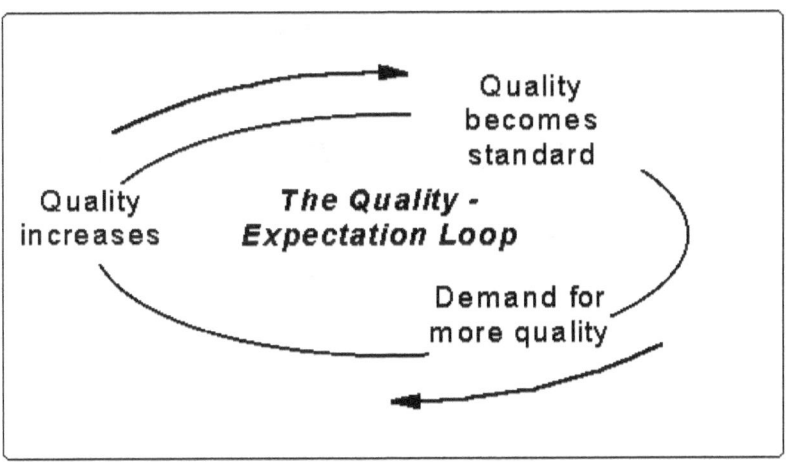

Figure 2-2: Quality Expectations

Peter Senge[18] demonstrates how a system is composed of a "circle of influence" connected through positive and negative feedback loops. He has established seven such archetypal circles. One of these archetypes can be applied to a very critical issue in government, the relationship

---

18 Senge, Peter, The Fifth Discipline: The Art of the Learning Organization

between revenues, citizen satisfaction, and service quality. Figure 2-3 shows that this relationship links one reinforcing and one balancing feedback loop so that the system's behavior is controlled by the balancing loop.

The chart is read as follows:

The balancing loop represents the relationship between revenue support (tax receipts) and the buying power of individuals. As buying power goes up, acceptance of taxing power goes up until a limit is reached whereby the amount of taxes collected negatively affects buying power. Then revenue support goes down until buying power is low enough to support an increase in revenue support again.

The reinforcing loop represents the relationship between the quality of service and program support (which also can be assessed in terms of revenues). As the quality goes up, individuals are willing to pay more for it. This would continue ad-infinitum, except that the balancing loop eventually interacts, reducing revenues, causing the quality of service to go down. That leads to a reduction in program support, ad-infinitum.

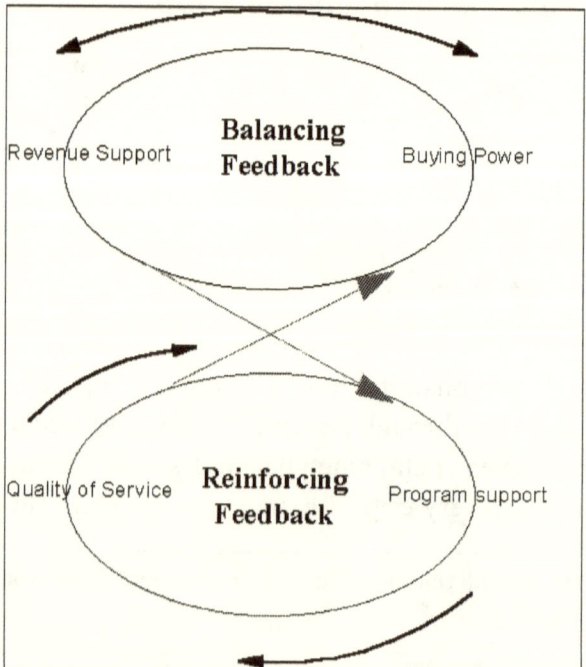

Figure 2-3: Feedback in Government Programs

Without the influence of the first loop, the reinforcing loop would always continue in one direction. Which direction (improved quality and support or decreasing quality and support) does not matter. Because there is nothing to stop the iterations, it is a reinforcing feedback loop.

Trying to understand the behavior of this system by breaking it into its two parts gives an inaccurate picture of what is happening. The critical issue here is to understand the overall qualitative system behavior, not the quantitative relationship of the parts. Such analyses can help an organization recognize barriers to effectiveness that are hidden under normal analysis.

The Basics of Complexity

Systems thinking exposes unexpected relationships. Unfortunately, the system can become too complex to provide useful information with standard analysis. As you will quickly recognize, some dynamics develop too many connections to allow for a true determination of cause and effect. In other cases, the time dimensions may become too broad to support causal claims. It is here where we must begin to consider the lessons of complexity.

There have been a number of discoveries in the science of complex systems which will eventually be applied to organizations. Seven of the discoveries appear to work together to form a comprehensive model of organizational behavior:

1) Simple nonlinear systems demonstrate complex behaviors: Complex nonlinear systems emerge from simple behaviors

2) Complex systems evolve from simplicity to greater complexity in response to increased complexity in their environment.

3)   Complex systems are dynamical, controlled by inherent structures while producing apparently random and unpredictable outputs.
4)   Complex systems build on reinforcing feedback.
5)   Complex systems are highly sensitive to small changes
6)   Complex systems are self-organizing.
7)   Complex systems can be controlled with chaos.

These seven discoveries all function on the other side of the barrier. Without them, the edge of chaos is a precipice of failure. With them it becomes possible to survive in a growing world of complexity.

Simple nonlinear systems demonstrate complex behaviors; complex nonlinear systems emerge from simple behaviors

Suppose you bring together a group of 100 people into a square 10 people by 10 people. Each person has two colored cards, one red and one blue. Each person is asked to hold up one card of his or her choice. From that point on, all participants obey the following three rules:

1)   if your neighbor to the left is showing a red card, continue to show the card you originally put up;
2)   If your neighbor to the left is showing a blue card, switch the cards in your hand;
3)   If you have no neighbor to the left, consider the individual at the far right end of your line as the person to your left. Continue changes unless the system reaches equilibrium (becomes all red).

Figure 2-4: Cellular Automata Randomly Stopped

Pretty simple system, right? Figure 2-4 shows a randomly picked point in time for a similar system. If you watched a system like this in motion, you would see the formation of images that appear to pursue and eat other images, form into alliances, distribute work, attack enemies, and other fascinating behaviors that simulate real life.

This example came from the mathematical construct called cellular automata. Does it apply in real life? Consider another set of three rules. A group of birds fly south each winter. Could their flocking behavior be defined by just three simple rules? The computer program called "BOIDS" demonstrates just such behavior. The three rules are:

    1)   Look around and decide where most other birds are and fly in their direction;

    2)   Try to match the velocity of the other birds; and

>   3)   Avoid bumping into each other and obstacles in their
>   paths.[19]

However, it still is not human. So, consider instead a lot of people driving their cars on an expressway. They all follow three rules: 1) drive at relatively the same speed; 2) keep a safe distance; and 3) try not to crash. (This is very similar to the BOIDS program.) When these three rules are modeled on a computer, a traffic jam forms at moderate levels of traffic flow, even when there is no accident to slow down and look at. The jam, called a soliton, flows against the direction of traffic until it works its way out of the group, when everything speeds up again.[20] Solitons were first identified in fluid mechanics. Its application to traffic patterns is just one example leading to understanding the role played by complex systems in the social sciences, another instance of the physical sciences leading to understandings in the social sciences.

Even the creation of personal values may be based on emergent rule behavior. For instance, Bernardo Huberman and Natalie Glance, at the XEROX Palo Alto Research Center have simulated the value of altruism on a computer. Their case goes like this. A work group decides to go out to lunch every Wednesday. They also agree that they will split the check evenly each week. How expensive will people's orders be over time relative to the cost of their co-worker's meals?

The problem for each individual to answer is, of course, should I get an expensive meal, since my cost will be averaged out, saving me money? Or should I be altruistic and try to help save money for the whole group? It turns out that, over time the ideal rule system that emerges from assuming selfish behavior is altruistic. Although individual actors will find that in the short term it may be to their benefit to purchase more expensive meals, cooperation saves the individuals money in the long term.[21]

---

19 Roetzheim, William H. *The Complexity Lab: Where Chaos Meets Complexity p 66*

20 Ibid. page 65

21 "Chaos and Cooperation", Glance, Natalie S and Huberman, Bernardo A, in *Chaos and Society*, A. Albert, ed.

A number of companies are beginning to develop and use software that relies on simple rules causing emergent complex behavior to improve production scheduling. Flavors Technologies, which was founded by Richard (Dick) Morley a number of years ago, created a production control system which is used in scheduling the Bullet Train in Japan, as well as in the truck body paint shop at General Motors Fort Wayne plant. The application of complexity theory will eventually impact a lot more than just business theory.

Complex Systems Evolve to Greater Levels of Complexity

All complex nonlinear systems appear to follow similar routes to complexification. According to chaotician Norman Packard, the generator of complexity is the need to process more complex forms of information. "Biological complexity has to do with the ability to process information. Computational capability, that's what we see in our cellular automata models, and in other complex adaptive systems. I view organisms as complex dynamical systems, and what drives their evolution is increased computational ability."[22]

Ralph Stacey explains that, as projections of biological systems, cultural artifacts such as organizations, community, society, and the global world order are all processes that have emerged to increase our ability to process information.[23] As such, they follow the same processes as biological systems in response to increasing loads of information. The goal, to match the level of complexity in the environment to the level within the system. Achieving the goal optimizes the system's ability to adapt to changes in the environment, thereby increasing its fitness. As we will see

---

22 In Lewin, Roger, Complexity: *Life at the Edge of Chaos*, p137,
23 Stacey, Ralph, Complexity and Creativity in Organizations.

later, this idea forms the basis of a new understanding of organizational learning and fitness.

Organizational complexification matches how biological systems evolve from simple to organisms that are more complex. The fertilized single cell egg of an animal is undifferentiated. It continues that way for a number of iterations, and then some border cells—responding to different chemical interactions at their place in the systems, differentiate. Eventually, through ongoing interaction between the boarder cells following a code of rules inscribed in the DNA which define how to respond under various conditions, and their embryonic environment, cells differentiate into skin, bones, eyes, brain matter, and all of the other components that make up the complete animal. No single cell is programmed to become skin or bones, specialization is the result of interaction between the cell and its environment.

Most organizations start with a founder/president or founders/board of directors. Assuming that the organization starts with little or no money, the president or, in the latter case the Chief Executive Officer begins performing the work of the organization. As revenues increase, the CEO hires an assistant to help perform the service or build the product—differentiation begins. Usually we see this process develop into the manufacturing or service delivery system of the organization. Once that part gets big enough, a second group of tasks, usually the financial tasks, become too cumbersome for the CEO alone. A new assistant to the CEO is hired who begins doing all this work—leading to development of the finance department. This process of complexification keeps repeating itself until we see formation of a mature organization with manufacturing (or service delivery), finance, marketing, and human resource management functions fully developed, plus more help to the CEO to manage the resulting increased flow of information. This is the process of complexification in organizations.

Even the mature organization continues to differentiate. As the company grows, manufacturing breaks up into product lines, finance breaks up into accounting, purchasing, investments, and growth continues. If the organization starts with lots of money, the process is truncated, but it still exists.

The process sounds very linear until we consider the changing lines of information flow for that organization. Karl Weber, the 19th century sociologist, gave us an image to attempt to maintain linearity—the bureaucracy. David Hurst[24] writes that the initial organizing process is chaotic, with little differentiating of roles and responsibilities. According to Hurst, Weber's departmental walls do not appear until the organization's orientation changes from development to performance.

Bureaucratic walls are always informally breached. Breaking the rules enables self-organization of more effective, and clearly nonlinear information flow patterns. These patterns become inscribed in the organization's grapevine and culture.

Through TQM and reengineering, organizations are consciously replacing bureaucratic walls with cross-functional project teams, work cell manufacturing, and other forms of organizational structure. Rather than simplifying the organization, these strategies are enabling smoother information flow within the more complex model.

As systems complexify, they also tend to reorganize. The types of cells found in a fertilized egg no longer exist in the full-grown animal. Organizational restructuring follows the same path. The obvious example is the CEO him/herself in the above example, acting as the fertilized egg verses being a part of the mature organizational neural system. A completely different set of skills, what we will explain as *holsight* in the Chapter 4, is needed for leading the mature organization.

---

24 Hurst, David, *Crises and Renewal.*

Complex Systems are Dynamical

There is an important distinction between a dynamic and a dynamical system. A dynamic system is one in which there is change—possibly continuous change. But there is a direct, predictable relationship between the input into the system and its outputs.

For instance, if the fictitious automobile company above builds 30 automobiles a day with 10 workers, in a dynamic system it is reasonable to predict that the agency can build 60 cars per day with 20 workers.

Reality and complex systems do not fit this mold. If the company wants to build 60 cars, it may do so with the same 10 workers by speeding up the line. Or, based on the first fundamental, the company will probably recognize after a short period of time that it needs an additional manager to keep things running smoothly (and, of course, an additional administrative assistant as well!), resulting in an increase to 22 workers. *A dynamical system is a system that changes but for which changes in outcomes appear to have no relationship to the changes in system input.*

We will explore the dynamics causing this apparent paradox later. For now, consider that this point confirms the reality that most managers have experienced all their life—*the plan almost never comes out as planned.*

If there appears to be no relationship between input and outcome, is this really a system? The answer is the amazing discovery that started the mathematical exploration of chaos. Although input and outcome differ, within a dynamical system lies a deep structure which defines the boundaries of the system's potential behavior.

The weather system provides a good way to demonstrate this structure. Forecasters have never been able to accurately predict weather more than 3 days ahead. The system is so complex that it is impossible to directly trace cause and effect. Ocean temperature and the location of the jet stream affect some large trends, but local conditions can offset those trends. While rain may be predicted for my area, I can (and have) seen a sunny day while there was rain to the north, east, south and west of me.

In the 1960s, the meteorologist Edward Lorenz discovered that within the mathematics of weather prediction lay an unexpected image of how the system changes *over time.* The image, which coincidentally looks like a butterfly (Figure 2-5), demonstrates the boundaries of system behavior. Lonrenz's discovery proved that accurate, local predictability of weather more than three days in advance is impossible. Yet this *strange* or *chaotic* attractor insures that it will not snow in Key West FL in June nor will there be 100-degree temperatures in Canada in December.

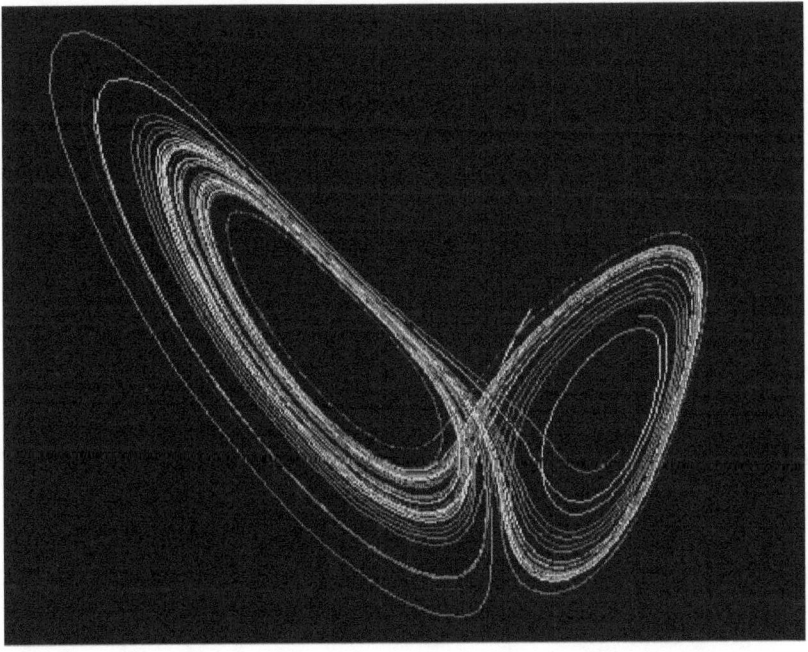

Figure 2-5: Lorenz's Chaotic "Butterfly" Attractor

Chaotic attractors are multi-dimensional time series graphs that plot changes in a given system over time. In Lorenz's butterfly attractor, the points on the graph represent the relationship of the outcomes of three nonlinear equations that control weather behavior, as those relationships evolve over time. Norman Packard and others found that it was possible to identify a dishonest roulette wheel and improve betting using real numbers from the wheel. Richard Priesmeyer experiments with real numbers representing various organizational relationships (like return on investment vs staffing levels), finding similar attractors in organizational behaviors.[25]

Chaotic attractors are one of three types of attractors associated with complex systems. A single-point attractor appears for systems whose behavior does not change. The single point represents the system's having reached equilibrium. A single-point attractor defines the behavior of a free-swinging pendulum. If you observe the logistics equation which previously was used to describe market conditions ($X_{n+1}=KX_n(1-X_n)$), for K values less than 3.0, (for instance, when there is little difference between supply and demand) you will see a single point attractor. The numbers of competitors will remain fairly stable.

On a traditional graph, (Figure 2-6, showing solutions of the Logistics Equation on a standard graph), outputs from such a stable system (Line K=2) will appear to have an initial wobble, followed by the results achieving a straight line. This demonstrates that there is no change in the system over time.

---

25 Priesmeyer, Richard. *Organizations and Chaos.*

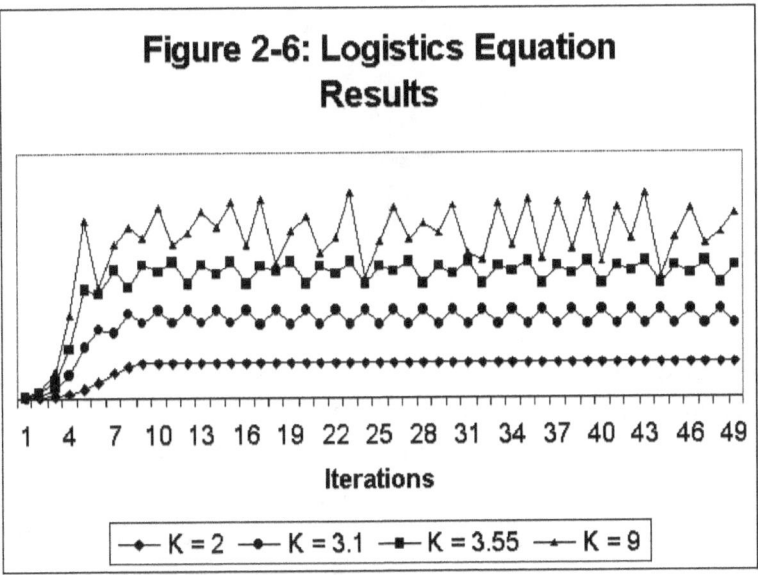

This system can also be demonstrated on a graph plotted to show the amount of change that happens from point to point over time.[26] Here the concept of attraction to the single point is clearly demonstrated as the graph moves from a point on the outside of the graph where the change in the amount of swing of the pendulum is large, until it stops moving at a single point. (Figure 2-7) No change is taking place, the system is dead in the water.[27]

---

26 This type of graph is called a phase space graph, and is critical to demonstrating the type attractors used in nonlinear systems. For a complete description of phase space, see Gleick.

27 We think of a system at equilibrium as stopped. But under this schema, we really mean that it is not changing behaviors. For instance, an engine running at 600 rpm for an hour has parts moving within the system, but the system's behavior has not changed. This would be confirmed in a phase space graph, which would look like the graph for the pendulum. Since most organizations have moving parts, it is important to understand that the organization is still at equilibrium. To help clarify the situation, I call this type of equilibrium "dynamic equilibrium".

Figure 2-7: Single Point Attractor in Phase Space

The second type of attractor, the *limit-cycle attractor*, develops for systems that repeat their patterns over time. Profits of a seasonal industry, such as snow sleds, exhibit a limit cycle for cash flow, with increasing cash in fall and winter, and declining cash in spring and summer.

When the logistics equation is set so that K is between 3.0 and 3.56, this appears as a repeating oscillation on the time series graph. Depending upon K, there may be single, double, quadruple, etc oscillations, but the line always repeats its pattern (Figure 2-6 where K=3.1 and K=3.55). The actual cycle is even more apparent when the system is displayed in a phase space graph such as the one used for the pendulum above (Figure 2-8).

Figure 2-8: Limit Cycle Example in Phase Space

The personal computer industry currently experiences this type of cycle. When the industry started around 1980, there were many different companies and platforms. Remember Kaypro and Columbia? Eventually, the number of companies narrowed to three major ones, IBM, Apple, and Compaq. As they raised prices, new competitors came into the market, followed by another retrenchment raising the new leaders as Packard Bell, Dell, Gateway, and Compaq. Hewlett Pakard, IBM. Toshiba, NEC, and Sony were struggling to stay in the market, and, as of this writing, Apple is being forced to consider joining the primary "WINTEL" platform. However, other processors that use technology similar to Intel, such as the AMD-K processor, are opening the way for another period of expansion.

The first group of major companies (IBM, Compaq, and Apple) probably felt smug following the first shakeout. They won the war and would live with skirmishes between themselves. Traditional management thinking failed to analyze market fluctuation beyond the initial upswing and consolidation—at least not until some young upstart like Dell successfully challenged them.

When K goes above 3.56 in the logistics equation, the system becomes chaotic. On a traditional, time series graph (Figure 2-6 where K=3.9), we see wild, unpredictable gyrations in outcomes. Everyone fears this chaos. However, we see a different image in phase space. Instead of apparent randomness, we see the emergence of a chaotic or *strange attractor* as previously shown in Figure 2-5. Chaotic attractors represent the inherent controls of the system that form the basis for self-organization and adaptation.

Eco-systems can move from cyclical to chaotic by introducing a new factor or variable into the system. For forty years, the eco-system in Yellowstone National Park was unstable as wolves disappeared from the environment. In 1992 wolves were reintroduced into the area. Now the system is re-stabilizing.

Priesmeyer showed that Toro Industries moved into the chaotic realm as a result of adding a product (snow blower) followed by a period of mild winters.[28] Our contention is that some parts of an organizational system are always in the chaotic realm, and that this is necessary to enable the organization to adapt and grow over time.

The logistics equation models only specific organizational behavior. Chaotic realms within organizations will exhibit different groups of attractors dependent upon the system variables involved. Different types of chaotic attractors have been generated from data from the commodities markets, from iterations of The Beer Distribution Game played at the Mass. Institute of Technology, and elsewhere.

The chaotic attractor distinguishes the difference between a dynamic and dynamical system. It does not exist in a dynamic system, where we have an identifiable relationship between input and output. For potential dynamical systems, the absence of a chaotic attractor would mean that no relationships exist within the system. That would be like a bunch of rocks that do not touch each other.

We are only at the infancy stage in our ability to map out attractors in organizational systems. They are clearly different from standard tools for leadership decision making. Instead of projecting potential futures, they demonstrate patterns of behavior that emerge over time. Many of our current analysis tools provide static images that represent single points in time. Dynamical systems analysis is like observing video instead of just a snapshot. As we will see later, it is the process of pattern recognition and creation that is central to learning, adaptation, and survival.

---

28 Ibid. pps, 54 - 56

Dynamical systems build on reinforcing feedback

The discussion on system dynamics explained the difference between balancing (controlling) and reinforcing (iteration) feedback. Balancing feedback exists to limit the impact of change that invades a system from its environment. A performance evaluation, for instance, is designed to keep the employee in line with the goals of the organization. An accounting system is designed to insure that the agency does not spend funds outside the limits of its revenues or approved funding categories.

Some of these balancing feedback tools and systems are necessary within organizations. But with rapid change needed to survive in turbulent environments, too much balancing feedback means certain death for an organization.

Reinforcing feedback means hearing the change that one's organization causes within its environment—as well as hearing other sources of environmental change, and adapting to that change. But reinforcing feedback causes chaos. We hear the chaos in the squelch that comes from a loud speaker when a microphone is held close to the speaker. If that is what management is about, who wants it?

Yet surprisingly, that squelch is produced by a dynamical system—there is a hidden structure within the squelch just like within other dynamical systems. Scientists find a rich world of organization within the squelch of a nature similar to that in the weather.

Reinforcing feedback can be viewed from a tamer perspective, information flow and discovery. Reinforcing feedback is the admittance of new information into a system concerning the system's environment.[29] In short, reinforcing feedback is the act of and action upon discovery.

---

29 The use of the word environment is for convenience sake. Later, we will see how the boundaries disappear between an organization and its environment, so that understanding the organization requires understanding its interactions with that environment.

One of the simplest yet most important examples of reinforcing feedback in organizations has to do with the organization's relationship to its environment. A simple description of the relationship goes like this: when an entity acts, it changes its environment. That change then feeds back to the first entity, causing it to change, causing the environment to change, etc.

A business example will make it clearer. (Figure 2-9) The auto industry began selling cars in the 1950s with air conditioners and radios sold as extras. To help sales, they began to offer package deals with the radios thrown in. Soon the consumer expected the radios as part of the standard equipment. So tape decks were sold as extras. These are now becoming standard, as is air conditioning. (The industry still shows air conditioning as extra on some price tags, but they build very few cars without them.) Now, power windows, once a status symbol of the rich, are moving into expected equipment.

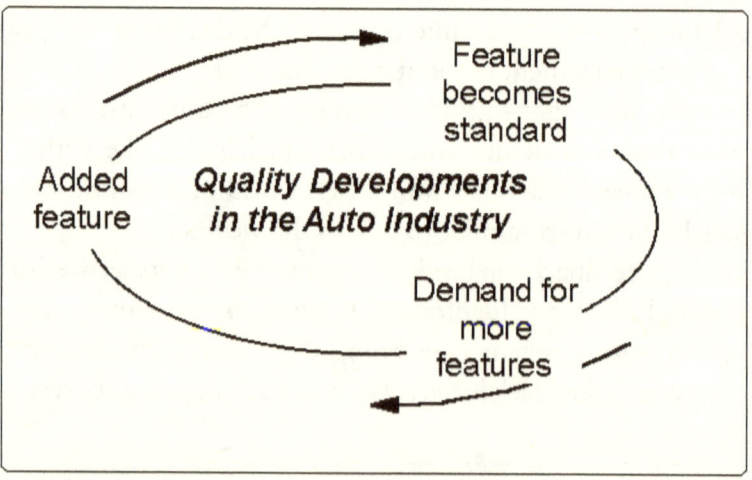

Figure 2-9: Equipment Expectations in the Automobile Industry

The health care industry experiences this same kind of reinforcing feedback loop as it develops new "cures" leading to an expectation of better care for all.

Organizational systems are also full of balancing feedback loops. What happens when the market place changes as it did for the auto industry in the 1970s? Or more interestingly, when the economy changes, or a major flood hurts the organization? The constellation of balancing loops makes it difficult for the agency to smoothly adapt to the changes. Without incorporating a method for allowing positive information to influence an organization, the organization will whither away and die.

Digital Equipment remains a prime example of this behavior. Digital's founder and former CEO, Ken Olsen, was so confident about his company's products and vision that employees were not given funds to attend trade shows except as exhibitors. Such shows were a major source of competitor and market information, and Digital failed to move as its market switched to different software platforms. Digital's case will be discussed throughout this book.

We call organizations that are strongly controlled by balancing feedback forces as equilibrium organizations. While many managers inherently value the idea of being at equilibrium—with everything running smoothly—in a complex world the word "equilibrium" means the same as death.

Systems require reinforcing feedback to change. Reinforcing feedback creates problems and conflict for organizations. *A problem exists when there is a difference between the current behavior of one part of a system with the behavior of another part.* For instance, a fast food company specializing in hamburgers has a problem when tastes move from hamburgers to family style dining. This was the problem facing MacDonalds shortly after Ray Kroc's death, leading to its experimenting with alternative menus and facility designs. Unfortunately, the balancing forces within McDonalds caused it to experiment with menus for too short a time. Now it is experimenting with types of facilities, and it is running into considerable resistance from traditional facility franchisers whose outdated facilities are threatened by the changes.

But a problem also exists when a customer comes in needing a service similar to your services but which your company does not provide. This is an example of problems developing on the microsystem level. One customer is not much of a problem. But when numerous customers come in with the same need, the problem can become overwhelming. If you do not find a way to serve them, they may go elsewhere, find a company that provides both services, and never return. They pass word along to other customers and your customer base shrinks along with your revenues. Eventually, your company dies. The stampede away from your company is a reinforcing feedback process, your company's reaction is controlled through balancing feedback systems.

A manager's typical response is to find ways to avoid problems, for instance by restricting "competition" between companies. Building in reinforcing feedback means searching out problems and addressing them as they happen. The search requires building new information routes into the organization and accepting and acting upon changes in the larger system. These routes form the positive feedback structures that take a system to the edge of chaos, where adaptation and survival are intertwined.

Continuous improvement, the type of quality management taught by the late W. Edwards Deming, is one piece of the puzzle for building positive feedback into organizational systems. A similar piece is Total Quality Service as proposed by Karl Albrecht. Both strategies involve discovering new information about the delivery of one's product (service) to its market place. The discovery process opens the organization to adaptation as the market changes.

An alternative form of quality management limits organizational growth and change. This is the system built on the concept of "benchmarking" and "zero defects." Both establish a static definition of planned outcomes based on what is known from the past, comparable practice and past consumer behavior. As consumer interests, technology, or other systems change, these changes are ignored as the practitioner attempts to maintain the parameters established in the past. Benchmarking and zero defect quality are negative feedback systems.

Dynamical systems are highly sensitive to small changes

Sensitivity to small changes is the generator of unpredictability in dynamical systems. It represents both the curse and blessing of the new science.

While identifying the chaotic attractor in the weather system, meteorologist Edward Lorenz also discovered the concept of sensitivity to initial conditions. His research may be the best way to describe what it means.

Lorenz developed a computer simulation of the global weather system in the 1960s. The simulation was based on the relationship between three nonlinear mathematical formulas. The computer processed the information at six decimal points, but reported the results at only three. According to the story, one day the computer broke down. Lorenz restarted the simulation from the point of collapse, except that he could only input the starting figure to the precision of three decimal points. [30]

Lorenz believed that the slight problem in accuracy would make no difference in his results. In fact, after following the original pattern for a

---

30 How little was this difference? To understand it, visualize the difference between a six decimal and three decimal number. The six decimal number inside the computer may be 0.111001. But the reported, three decimal number is 0.111. The amount of difference between the two numbers is only 0.000001!

short time period, the new run radically diverged from the first. Eventual review of his findings led to the recognition that, at least for weather systems, a very small change in starting conditions—such as a butterfly flapping its wings in Argentina—will grow into a major and unpredictable difference in the system outcome, like a thunderstorm over the Mid West. In recognition of the discovery, it is frequently referred to as the "butterfly effect." (By the way, Lorenz's discovery explains why it will be impossible to accurately predict local weather more than three days in advance. No one has yet figured out, however, why weather can't seem to be predicted accurately overnight, either!)

You probably recognize that the butterfly effect is another version of Murphy's Law—"what ever can go wrong in a system, will go wrong in that system." It is the generator of the law. More importantly, it is the generator of unpredictability and surprise. The butterfly effect is the generator of the kind of chaos that most of us work so hard to avoid.

The problem is demonstrated in the Beer Distribution Game described by Senge. The simulation is set up on what appears to be a simple, straightforward distribution system. Each team includes five people representing different parts of the distribution chain: the store owner who orders the beer; three distributors who pass the orders up the line and the beer back down through the system; and the factory which brews and originally ships the beer. The store owner orders beer based upon current inventory and sales each week, which s/he learns about from a deck of cards. Each other position orders from above based upon the individual's perception of what will be needed in the future. It takes four moves of the game for the storeownr's first order to impact the factory, and four more moves before the order is actually fulfilled. Communication is only through the distribution line, the store owner cannot deal directly with the factory.

In the game, there is only one change in the number of beers ordered from the store—a jump in the standard order is made in the fourth round of the game. But the result is always disaster to the unexpecting participants, as they vary their orders at each level into a wild, gyrating system.[31]

Anyone who has gone into chaos playing The Beer Distribution Game, or who has experienced a system that went over the edge, will be highly skeptical about any suggestion that organizations should not back away from the edge of chaos. Although scientists used to have the same concerns, the situation there is quickly changing. And that change will radically alter how we lead our organizations.

The most obvious "negative" implication of this discovery on organizations is the impact of the butterfly effect on one's capacity to plan. In essence, the butterfly effect means that long range planning is virtually impossible. Traditional management acts as though one can establish a long range plan followed by small changes to keep the plan functional. But a small change, whether planned or serendipitous, will blossom into unpredictable large scale change some time down the road, steering the organization in an unexpected direction. As a result, even the *traditional definitions and functions of vision and mission become inapplicable to effective leadership in complex organizations.*

Some entrepreneurs demonstrate an instinctive understanding of the butterfly effect. People like, Jeffrey Glicksman, who founded Spyglass, gave their company room to move. Spyglass' first product was Thumbscan, an invention for personal identification based on thumb print recognition. The company moved on to develop products under contract for federal agencies. Then it moved into a battle for supremacy in cyberspace with its licensing of Mosaic, the first web-based Internet access tool, which was later licensed to Microsoft and evolved into the

---

31 For a complete description of **The Beer Distribution Game**, see Senge, Peter, *The Fifth Discipline, The Art of the Learning Organization.* For a discussion of the nonlinear aspects of the game see, Mosekilde, Erik and Larsen, Erik Reimer. "Deterministic chaos in the Beer Production-Distribution Model", System Dynamics Review (4)1 & 2 pps 132–147; and , Michaels, Mark, "The Beer Distribution Game: A Second Look", *The Chaos Network Newsletter* (5)1

Microsoft Internet Explorer. The company thrived until it settled down on Mosaic as its mission. Linked into the battle against Netscape, the new leaders at Spyglass undersold the license for Mosaic to Microsoft, taking the company into an eventual tailspin. Spyglass, no longer under Glicksman's leadership, was no longer in a position to adapt.

This radical revolution about planning is so important that it will be discussed in detail in Chapter 3.

For now, let's consider the other side of this concept. If a small change can blossom into unpredictable large-scale change, we can also leverage small changes to the benefit of the organization.

Most organizational change efforts are large scale, top down efforts. But they are not really transformations. They represent the killing of old organizations and birthing of new ones—under the name of the old. Such changes involve the termination of many employees who do not have the skills for the new business, and the hiring of others who do fit in. In complexity terms, the organization experiences a catastrophic or discontinuous change on the scale of the end of the age of dinosaurs.

The few successful large scale change efforts actually only institutionalize incremental change that has developed over a period of time. The ability to make change stick represents a longer history than is generally recognized during the effort. Chapter 5 will explore how the butterfly effect allows for multi-directional, evolutionary, though unpredictable change. Such change starts with the recognition that there is always a pool of small changes going on throughout the organization. This develops from the diversity within the organization, and the many, unofficial experiments generated by diverse thinkers. Other changes may develop from smaller, "planned" changes or even from errors that develop in the course of every day life. The total configuration of the potential for change can be called the *random repertoire of possibilities*.

Small change also develops in the organization's environment. Eventually, one or more of the organizational differences may link with changes in the environment. A new, reinforcing feedback loop emerges.

Eventually, if there is sufficient change in the environment, this new function builds into either a second organizational function or, potentially, becomes the core business if the original function has died.

This is the strategy in place at 3M Company. The company always has a number of potential products on the drawing boards, enabling new products to fill in the gap as market conditions change. 3M's product diversity reduces its dependence upon any one market sector, and enables periodic spectacular successes like the Post-It note to emerge.

Dynamical systems are self-organizing

Place a handful of spaghetti in a pot of boiling water. Once the spaghetti softens, the strands will form themselves into a donut shape, even while the individual strands move randomly within the shape. This is the optimal systemic relationship for cooking spaghetti. And it is an example of self-organization.

Place two water coolers at opposite ends of a large office. If you suspend a stop-action or video camera from the ceiling and keep it running for a number of weeks, you will see movement patterns relating to the coolers emerge. Most likely, the patterns will be based on the distance each individual is from any given cooler. Those closer in to a given cooler will restrict themselves to that one cooler more than those further away.

More interestingly, if you then study communication and decision patterns within the larger group, they will tend to be representative and supportive of the movement patterns. The one exception, those individuals who are farthest from all coolers will have the most interactions between the groups, becoming the intermediaries—information conduits—between groups. These individuals are on the borders. To the extent that they interact with other groups, the boundaries are open and reinforcing feedback loops may develop. To the extent that the group frowns on such interaction, the boundaries close and balancing feedback (peer pressure) closes off the group.

The water coolers act as attractors. Those using the coolers work within the basins of attraction. The system has, over time, self-organized, and the self-organization will have a major impact on the operations of a company, establishing the corporate culture, decision structure, and informal information system within the group.

The process of self-organization is surprisingly orderly. Those theoreticians who tinker with artificial life simulations have found a number of routes to self-organization. The process will be explored in detail in Chapter 6.

Controlling chaos with chaos

Self-organization happens at all levels of organization, from small group interactions to relationships with the market place, industry, etc. But it emerges only when constraints (balancing feedback) are not built in. Such constraints are typical of management. Organizations attempt to thwart the flow of self-organization because the potential results will not fit in a pre-defined plan. The basic methodology is to control chaos with balancing feedback systems such as management by objectives and performance evaluation.

Complexity theory recognizes that this attempt to control chaos with traditional (balancing feedback) methods is a recipe for failure. Alfred Hubler, a chaotician at the University of Illinois, demonstrates this in his studies on the control of chaos.[32] Hubler's research shows that attempts to control chaos in systems by use of balancing feedback takes the system

---

32 Hubler, Alfred, "The Control of Chaos" *Proceedings of the 3rd Annual Chaos Network Conference*, Michaels, Mark, ed.

out of contact with its environment. Eventually, a strain builds up (problem) between the needs of the environment and the system. Instead of a smooth transition, the strain produces periodic catastrophes.

Stephen Jay Gould and others studying biological evolution, describe a similar process as punctuated equilibrium.

Hubler's work has an optimistic side, demonstrating a way to potentially avoid such catastrophes. Hubler shows that chaos can be controlled with weak chaos. One of Hubler's favorite examples of how chaos controls chaos is to show a randomly dripping faucet under a strobe light (the light making it easier to see the randomness of the drips.) Hubler attaches a vibrator that provides a mild, yet random vibration, to the faucet. All of a sudden, the drips become highly regular.

Unfortunately, many leaders misunderstand the concept of controlling chaos. Here, Hubler is using what he calls "weak chaos." The difference between weak and strong chaos is mathematically derived. We find weak chaos on the logistics map at the area ranging from about $K=3.56$ to 3.9. After that, the results are pure randomness.

Metaphorically, the difference can best be described in Hubler's words. He explains that strong chaos is like hitting a pendulum made of china with a large, metal mallet. Weak chaos is like taking a rubber mallet and periodically tapping a wooden pendulum with it.

Peters, in *Thriving on Chaos*, failed to differentiate between these to levels of chaos. Peters' proposed that one way to build loyalty and alignment with the organization was to create a sense of urgency within the organization. Even if the ship wasn't sinking, Peters challenged leaders to make like it was. Peters has continued this prescription for strong chaos in his latest book, *The Circle of Innovation*, where he professes that "Destruction is cool!"[33]

A striking example of the results of misunderstanding this dynamic resulted in the Persian Gulf War. The cause of that war was Saddam

---

33 Peters, Tom, The Circle of Innovation: *You Can't Shrink Your Company to Greatness.*

Hussein's attempt to break the equilibrium state of relations between the oil producing countries by instilling an act of strong chaos into the system. His goal was to take advantage of the "chaos" to improve his own country's status within that system. The result was the response by those involved in and benefiting from equilibrium joining forces to maintain equilibrium conditions.

Most leaders fail to understand the distinction between weak and strong chaos. Instilling unrelated chaos, such as forced job transfers and reorganization—periodically shaking things up—has the same effect on an organization as the metal mallet on a china pendulum. Employees react negatively to such chaos, eventually burning out from the meaningless change. Over time, the organization falls apart.

Weak chaos exists at the edge of chaos. This is the place where a resonance develops between the organization and its environment. Weak chaos is inherent within organizations. It is the diversity of thought, the "errors against plan," the absences from scheduled meetings. It is also the new ideas, the "skunk works" projects, and the information obtained from attending a conference. Such information is useless if balancing feedback dampens its impact. Given a chance to iterate, weak chaos enables the building of linkages with environmental changes, resulting in adaptation and survival.

Quality management, defined as continuous improvement, is one way to bring weak chaos into an organization. Quality management requires that organizational members, usually the Continuous Improvement Teams, seek out and process new information. Team members are given tools to help sift through the extensive amount of information available to determine when to experiment. Then, their role is experimentation—trying new ideas out on the small scale first, and then to iterate the successes into organizational change. The "Plan-Do-Check-Act" process is one such technique.

Conclusion

I remember a movie when I was growing up called, "Breaking the Sound Barrier." In the movie, a number of test pilots failed to break the sound barrier because weird things, like a severe rattle developing in the control stick, would happen at speeds close to Mach 1. According to the movie, the pilot who finally broke the barrier, Chuck Yeager, did so by reversing the controls—doing everything backwards.

Yeager denies the story in his autobiography. But the lesson holds for breaking through the barriers at the edge of chaos. As systems speed up and become complex, we will have to reverse our approach to business. We will have to learn to instill weak chaos into our systems, instead of finding ways to protect ourselves from the unpredictability of change.

Once at the edge of chaos, many options exist. Depending upon the situation, one or another option may be preferable. The only way to find the best option is through trial and error—through exploring the landscape around you. As the rest of this book emerges, we will see that such explorations are not a matter of vision, but of holsight.

Another popular cultural phenomenon in my youth was the television show *Get Smart*. Maxwell Smart was a secret agent who fought against the evil machinations of C.H.A.O.S. on behalf of his organization, C.O.N.T.R.O.L. Smart's responsibilities echo those of today's managers, and the mess-ups that he always experienced demonstrate the problems associated with how managers control chaos. Those who grasp an understanding of this book will quickly agree, Maxwell Smart worked for the wrong team.

Chapter 3

Fitness: The Goal of Strategy

The most glaring distinction between traditional strategy and strategy in complex environments is the role played by vision. Vision is now practiced as the first step in almost any major planning process. That is because the traditional planning process involves deciding where you want to be and making a plan to get there.

It is interesting to note that, of all the ways in which the brain senses the environment, we have emphasized the visual senses in the choice of the term vision. We do not talk about an organization's taste, smell, or sound. There is a little thought about the feel (touch) of an organization coming from marketing people. But the organization's vision has become the paramount sensation.

Vision is not something in the here and now. It is always related to seeing down a path, to seeing into the future, to creating a future.

How did visioning become such an important part of the leadership process? A brief characterization of the history of leadership will help.

Many of the following assumptions are based on Julian Jaynes enlightening work on the nature of the mind. Jaynes proposes that early humans acted more in concert with and in direct response to their immediate environments then is the practice of the modern Homo sapien. As is assumed about consciousness in other animals, there was neither time perspective nor intentionality.[34] That could only develop once humans were able to distinguish between themselves and their environment. This was true, according to Jaynes, beyond about 6000 years ago.

In the extended period of pre-history prior 4000 BC, leaders were not visionaries. They were problem solvers in exactly the meaning of the term problem that we are using in this book. If they or others sensed a change in the tribe's environment—which usually meant a threat to the tribe's survival—the leader either directly or with the support of others, responded to the problem. This enabled the tribe to survive.

Survival also meant acquiring scare resources to feed the tribe. Both tasks, defense and resource acquisition, required strength. So the tribe selected its strongest person as the leader.

Jaynes describes the development of visionaries beginning around 3 thousand years ago (early Egypt and Mesopotamia) as this so-called bicameral mind which unified human kind with its environment, breaks down. This, I feel, lead to the first iteration of leadership.

Back then, the leader's primary role remained insuring the survival of the tribe. However, the tribe and its competitors became more numerous as social groups switched from foraging to farming. Survival could not be achieved with just the leader's strength. Survival required garnering the physical strength of a collective body. The leader needed the capacity to foster collective strength even when the required individual behavior might be contrary to the interests of that individual. The leader's own strength, directed at fellow tribesmen, provided some help in this capacity. But the visionary divination of what was ordained in destiny provided strong support for this power.

At that time, vision was, very simply, *a prediction of the future environment and the status of the group in that environment, which was supposedly*

---

34 Jaynes, Julian. *The Origin of Consciousness and the Breakdown of the Bicameral Mind*

identified through an understanding of destiny. The vision provided direction for the group's action.

Early visionaries were scary individuals. A prophet of wealth or doom, the visionary's actions appeared otherworldly. In a predetermined world, the visionary appeared to have the power of insight into retribution if crossed. The visionary did not create the future. S/he identified the predetermined direction of the future, told the people what must be done to survive in line with the gods' plans, and the consequences for not aligning with destiny.

The Hebrew prophets predicted catastrophe if the leader (the anointed king) was not followed, at least so long as the king modified the decisions of passed leaders incrementally instead of massively. Any major deviation from past decisions was always confronted with terror of retribution. During the exile of the Israelites, the prophet provided hope if the group continued to follow the direction of the previously anointed leaders.

With the exception of the Hebrew patriarchs, this visionary was not the leader. Leadership remained in the hands of the strongest individual—who still could chop off the head of a wayward visionary. (Consider the fate of John the Baptist!) But the visionary served the leader by motivating the tribe to action when such was necessary in response to real or perceived (by the visionary) threats. This seems true whether the visionary was Murdoch or Merlin, and whether the leader was a Babylonian or King Arthur.

Beginning a couple of hundred years before the Common Era, a second type of prophet emerged. Buddha, Mohammed, the later Hebrew prophets and early rabbis, Jesus, and others broke from the Greek tradition of destiny, and established the ability for individual action.[35] At this turn, free will became tempered with values, with codes of behavior such as Rabbi Hillel's rendition of the golden rule—"do not do unto

---

35 Armstrong, Karen. *A History of God: The 4000 Year Quest of Judaism, Christianity and Islam*

others as others as you would not have others do unto you." These values were the guarantor of survival—to follow them meant walking in God's footsteps, and assured survival in this world (Judaism) or resurrection in another world (Christianity). Interestingly enough, this seems to be a period of reduced reliance of leadership, as individual actions led to personal relationships with the deity and survival. With the breakdown of the bicameral mind, we see the development of individual vision, action and responsibility.

A new iteration, re-establishing and merging leadership with autonomy, seems to have developed in the modern era. The visionary and the leader have merged. And the effectiveness of visions to unify the tribe has reached the point to preclude the need for the leader to appear physically strong. As tribes have moved more closely together, to some extent leadership has become a symbiotic relationship. We claim to follow leaders whose visions reflect our beliefs regarding our needs for survival. Thus, some leaders now must market their visions.

To achieve leadership today, the leader's vision is often couched in positive instead of retributive terms. George Bush's alleged problem with the "vision thing" was really a problem of communicating a positive image of the role of the US government in the minds of the constituency such as was done by Ronald Reagan. A number of commentators pointed out that Bush did have a vision of limited government and a free market place.

In business, many entrepreneurial leaders working in hi-tech areas have visions related to "creating a global network of people." These visions differ between entrepreneurs only in their reflection of the means for achieving them (value systems) and, thereby, the methods for insuring that group's survival.

Originally, conflict occurred between tribes when there was competition over a limited resource needed by each tribe or one tribe saw the other as a potential resource. With the second iteration, conflict occurs when the leaders represent contrary visions of what is required for survival or the visions indicate a need for limited, overlapping resources.

Consider, for instance, how the cold war was a battle between the vision of capitalistic/democratic values, which the "free world's" leadership believed was required for survival, and the central-control/socialistic vision held by the communist leaders. Both saw their vision as the best hope for survival of their tribe. Similarly, the "cola wars" between Coke and Pepsi, is a battle for survival where overlapping resources—market share—are required to insure the survival of each tribe, the Coke stakeholders and the Pepsi stakeholders.

The original leader used strength to defend the tribe and garner resources. With the first iteration, this strength became a function of the group. The leader used power to insure group cohesion and support of the vision. By the second iteration, the tone of power had broadened from autocratic to humanistic. But power management continued as a leadership role. However, such power acts contrary to the humanistic view, often leading to interesting contradictions of behavior.

This history brings us to the present time. Here we see that the two cornerstones of leadership, vision and power, will no longer succeed in assuring the survival of the tribe.

Vision, as you will recall, was defined as *a prediction of the future environment and the status of the group in that environment which provided direction for the group's action.* The problem, prediction of outcomes is both impossible for and potentially dangerous to a complex system.

Types of Visions Today

We still see artifacts of all three iterations of vision in our current leadership strategies. A vision may be:
- A prediction of the future environment and preferred position of the individual/organization within that environment.

- A constellation of personal or group values which the individual or group uses to define how it wishes to operate. Usually these values represent how the group would like to see it's world operate in the future as well.
- A desired future state that the leader hopes to achieve regardless of the current state of reality.

Predictive vision refers back to the oldest definition relating to the actions of prophets, shaman, medicine men, the Oracle of Delphi, and others. The phenomena is clearly traced and discussed in Jaynes' book.

The Old Testament, in particular, talks about visions by such prophets as Ezekial and Nehemiah. Because the culture (and language) of the time was so different than ours, we cannot be certain as to what role such visions took within the culture. Some appear to have been allegorical lessons (expressing values) while others actually predicted wealth and success. We also know that many prophetic statements—primarily those that failed, were not remembered, just like today when no one bother's to check last January's National Enquirer to keep a track record on the predictive success of self-professed modern "prophets" like Jean Dixon.

Predictive visions are predictions of system outcomes. They are usually in the form of "if x then y". "If the Israelites repent (return to the ways of the Lord), forego food, and wear ashes, they will return from the exile to the Promised Land." "When the Moon is in the seventh house and Jupiter aligns with Mars, then peace will guide the planets, and love will rule the stars." If you work hard on earth, you will reap rewards on both earth and in heaven. " Through this plan we will increase our market share to thirty percent in 3 years.

The only difference between biblical and modern prophecy is methodology. Where as the prophets used their divining rods and crystal balls, modern futurists use their spread sheets, regression and factor analysis. Both are based on the same assumption—that there is a route from point A to point B, and it is a straight line.

Successful predictions of system outcomes result from the interaction of two phenomena. First, prediction requires that a system be deterministic—that there is a predefined, direct route from point A to point B. In other words, the system's outcomes are defined by its known starting conditions. For instance, within a vacuum, one can predict the landing point of an arrow with knowledge of its starting position, trajectory, and velocity.

Some chaotic systems are deterministic. This was, in fact, one of the surprising discoveries of chaos theory. A complex system's outcomes are generally determined by its starting conditions.

However, a successful prediction requires being able to accurately determine the system's starting conditions—to know the location of point A, otherwise its location in the plan is meaningless. How accurate must this be? For linear systems, reasonably accurate is enough. In linear systems, a small difference in the system's starting position results in a comparably small difference in the system's outcome. If I drive from Newark NJ to Boston MA as if I drove from Manhattan to Boston and had exactly the right amount of gas to get from the Manhattan exit of the Lincoln Tunnel to Faneuil Hall, I would run out of gas at the start of Boston's South Station Tunnel, right before reaching downtown. Reasonably close descriptions of starting conditions will result in reasonably accurate predictions of outcomes.

In a complex, nonlinear system, a small difference in a system's starting position can result in a massive difference in the system's outcomes because of the constraint described in Chapter 2 called the Butterfly Effect.

A simple game of pool is frequently used to demonstrate deterministic chaos. A pool game starts with the break, during which the cue ball is shot at the 15 balls lined up in a triangle. The slightest change in the location of the target balls or trajectory of the cue ball will result in the balls breaking differently each opening shot. The resulting second shot may be only slightly different. But that difference is further magnified on the third and subsequent shots, until game two is radically different than game one.

How small a difference in the start will result in great, unpredictable differences in outcome? As Edward Lorenz first demonstrated upon discovering the Butterfly Effect, the difference is infinitesimally small. Since, by definition, an infinitesimal difference cannot be measured, it is impossible to identify the system's starting position. Therefore, even though the system's outcomes are determined by the starting position, because we don't know point A, we can't identify point B.

Prigogine questions whether assuming determinism in chaos causes the new science to be guilty to the linearity of Newtonian science, pointing out that it eliminates the impact of free will on the system. For Prigogine, the problem is that determinism assumes a single trajectory from a single point, but that multiple trajectories are possible from a single point. This, of course, further destroys the potential of predictability within complex systems.[36]

The majority of vision/mission statements appear to fit the idea of predictive vision. They are the statements that Brenda Zimmerman calls "simple and explicit".[37] Ralph Stacey recognizes that for an expert pool player, the short term results of the break are predictable, enabling short term planning, while the impact of sensitive dependence makes long term planning—visioning, impossible.[38] However, no one involved in complex systems theory appears to be arguing that long term predictive visions are viable on their own within the context of this theory.

The work of modern day prophets like Faith Popcorn and John Naisbitt is based on the idea that we can know point A and a few intermediary points, from which we can draw a straight line to find point B. Since their predictions are made in a nonlinear world, their assumptions

---

36 Prigogine, Ibid.
37 Zimmerman, Brenda. "The Management of Boredom"
38 Stacey, Ralph. *Managing the Unknowable*

and methodology do not hold up any better than the crystal ball. Most effective futurists (professional forecasters) now recognize this problem and do multiple scenario projections instead of predictions.

The idea of **vision as values** is almost as old as its predictive use. Reconsider biblically inspired statements, "If you love your neighbor, you will inherit the kingdom of heaven." Just as with predictive vision, the statements can be re-read to mean that practicing values X leads to future state Y.

The claim that following certain behaviors will lead to a New World Order is, in fact, a basic message of most religions. A given religion's vision of heaven is frequently that religion's picture of the preferred value and behavior structure on earth.

Theologians explain this role of vision as the quest for the transcendent. The role of the transcendent is, in modern times, the society's creation of a vision of a future, which supposedly pulls the society out from its present conditions. It is what the society strives for, and in striving, the society is, supposedly, pulled toward that future.

My preference is to call something what it is, so values should be called values. However, given the historical precedence linking values to vision, the issue should be addressed from a more objective standpoint. Doing so leads us to evaluate two issues:

- Whether the claim that values X will lead to a future state Y is the same linear mathematical formula found in predictive visions; and
- Whether recent theories describing the nature of change negates the effectiveness of the theoretical role of the transcendent in change processes.

The first issue should be easy to dismiss, but habits die hard. Demonstrating the values issue as another form of the "if X then Y" equation should result in its abandonment. Consider the absurdity of the examples on both the personal and organizational level.

Personal: "Do not do unto others as you would not have others do unto you." "Make a constructive contribution to society. You will reap what you sow." For those who are religious, these and similar values are supposed to be rewarded either here, which helps create a heaven on earth, or in heaven. I won't argue whether heaven exists, only that as many get rewards on earth for following such values as those who don't. The distribution of resources remains relatively random. Good people are killed in Bosnia and other war zones, die in floods in India and the Midwest, and in earthquakes in Japan and elsewhere, while "bad" people survive such catastrophes—and vice versa.

Organizational: Tom Peters wrote a ground breaking book in 1980 that is still considered a classic. *In Search of Excellence* developed a series of behaviors (values) for companies and leaders to follow. The list was developed from a survey of a group of companies that fit a series of exceptional performance criteria including longevity as leaders in the markets. Two years later, Business Week magazine reported that half of these "excellent" companies no longer fit the excellent criteria. And a number had, in fact, gone out of business.

More recently, studies of Baldrige Award winning companies have shown that many of these companies experience severe economic problems in the years following receipt of the award. These are cases in which companies are following what are considered to be the "best practices" in their industries, only to see negative results.

The same problem arises with leadership models based on the list of current, top corporate leaders. My guess is that you are already thinking about Tom Peters, Stephen Covey and others saying, "but look at all the successful leaders who started with a vision!" The answer is that their research methodology is faulted. All the studies are of successful leaders. No studies have been done of failed leaders, and the vast majority of corporate leaders have been involved in failed companies. Simple math will quickly demonstrate that more leaders who have used these values have failed then the number of those who succeeded.

These examples are a wake-up call to eliminate the formula created by the link of vision and values. This does not mean that values are not important in and of themselves. Values represent the contract made within a group that defines the behavior expected of its members. But for the most part, values emerge in response to the needs of the group in the context of its environment. They, like other aspects of a system, change, depending upon the demands of the environment—so long as a process exists which tolerates such change.

What gets our species into more trouble than a lack of values is linking the universal expectation of success to a group of values and imposing such linkage on others. Those groups that commit to a rigid set of values are the ones that eventually fall by the wayside. The reasons behind this will be discussed in detail in Chapter 6.

Having taken away the linkage between values and a predictable future, we are faced with the idea of the transcendent—an envisioned, desirable future—pulling us to that future. This process has been translated into management as organizational transformation—creating a vision of the future that draws the organization towards that future, and then developing a plan (mission) to achieve immediate movement towards that future.

The notion of the transcendent is religious in nature. This transference of religious processes into corporate behavior is resulting in some religions questioning whether organizations are trying to supplant religious belief. For those who attempt to practice congruent behavior, conflicts between the two visions can develop and result in real cognitive dissonance.

The use of vision (the transcendent) for organizational change can be understood as an adaptation of Kurt Lewin's force field theory of change. Lewin's change theory is based on the clearly linear formula F_E $+F_R=0$, where F_E are forces enabling change and F_R are forces resisting change. Lewin's thesis, upon which most of organization development is based, was that if the change agent alters the relationship of the two forces, the system will burst out of equilibrium, allowing change to begin. The result developed into the process of vision/mission/action planning, with vision being the process of increasing the enabling forces for change.

Jeffrey Goldstein has demonstrated that Lewin's formula is not applicable to complex, chaotic systems.[39] Lewin is correct to say a group that is not ready to change is at equilibrium. But there are better formulas to describe what that means. The logistics formula, first introduced in Chapter 2, is a model of how major change comes through iteration of small changes over time, rather than through the draw of an outside end state.

The failure of visionary leadership has become apparent to many leadership theorists. A new response is developing based on the notion that the leader's role is to **create one's own reality.** The response is developing from research into quantum mechanics.

Quantum mechanics, the study of the smallest particles in the universe, began early this century. The discipline recognizes that there is inherent chaos at the quanta (most minute) level of reality. As Prigogine explains, it uses Newtonian methodologies to study this chaos.[40]

Three interpretations of discoveries of quantum mechanics have impacted discussions of management theory:

- The observer of an experiment affects the result of that experiment. Theoretically, quanta can be observed as particles or waves. Early interpretations of this phenomenon assumed that it is the action of the observer that determines whether quanta are being observed as a particle or a wave.
- The observer can measure either the speed or direction of a particle but never both at the same time.

---

39 Goldstein, Jeffrey, *The Unshackled Organization*
40 Prigogine, Ibid.

- When two particles of different "spin" come in contact with each other, their spins coordinate. From that time forward, if the spin of one changes, the spin of the other changes at the same time, even though the two are not in physical contact with each other. Further, the change occurs immediately (faster than the speed of light, in fact).

When combined, nonscientists are observing that the results suggest a chaotic, non-substantive universe whose substance is produced by the observer. In other words, individually, we make our own worlds. The concept is supported by the suggestion that individuals who mentally imagine performing a future task before undertaking that task will perform the task better than those who just do it.

The application of this interpretation of quantum mechanics to visioning has been that the individual is responsible for the creation of one's own universe. That is, as the fictional creator of Jurassic Park explained in both the book and movie while his empire was crumbling around him, "I was always raised to believe that if you believe in something hard enough and work hard enough for it, it will come true."

There are a number of problems with this theory. The most important, that the integration of complexity theory with quantum mechanics has demonstrated that we do not create our own realities. Those studying quantum chaos, including Prigogine, are solving the wave/particle duality issue. They have demonstrated that mass is an emergent property that develops from system interaction independent of observer participation. Ferris explains that a researcher's choice to study quanta as a wave or a particle does not change the functioning of the quanta, which acts as both. We just do not have a better way to describe this pre-matter substance at this time. [41]

---

41 Prigogine presented his proof at a lecture at the University of Illinois, April 17, 1992. For an excellent discussion of the current interpretations of the "weirdness of quantum mechanics, see Chapter 11 in Ferris.

Scientists have again explained what common sense tells the rest of us: when I bang my head against the wall, it does hurt. If reality could be converted into a wave, the pain would go away and I'd stick my head through the wall without harming my head or the wall.

One strategy used to support this ill-advised notion is the practice of mental imaging. Brain research shows that imaging helps build the neural pathways that enable appropriate muscle response for performing a task. It is practice without practicing. Studies have demonstrated that the field goal kicker really does do better if he first envisions kicking the ball.

For long term tasks where the environment is steady, it might be possible to apply this visioning strategy to a series of tasks with some success. However, our current method is to do so for longer time frames and then fight like mad, as did the entrepreneur in *Jurassic Park*, to make sure the environment stays as we planned. Thanks to the dreams of others and Mother Nature, it turns out that the environment is really something we can't control. Just consider the field goal kicker who uses positive imaging. His image has the ball flying between the goal posts every time, and the process may have worked the last 10 kicks. But along comes an unexpected gust of wind and the ball veers quickly to one side. For most companies, today, the wind is always blowing.

Probably the best way to understand the fallacy of this leadership theory is with the following mind game. Simply picture ten entrepreneurs creating their own realities. What happens when Entrepreneur 3 creates a reality in conflict with Entrepreneurs 1 and 5. If they can all create their own realities and, therefore, they can all succeed, then than each entrepreneur must live in a parallel universe. However, although we now assume multiple universes, the theory of parallel universes has generally been rejected. If it were true, however, why should I slave under Entrepreneur 7's vision when he can be my slave under my vision?

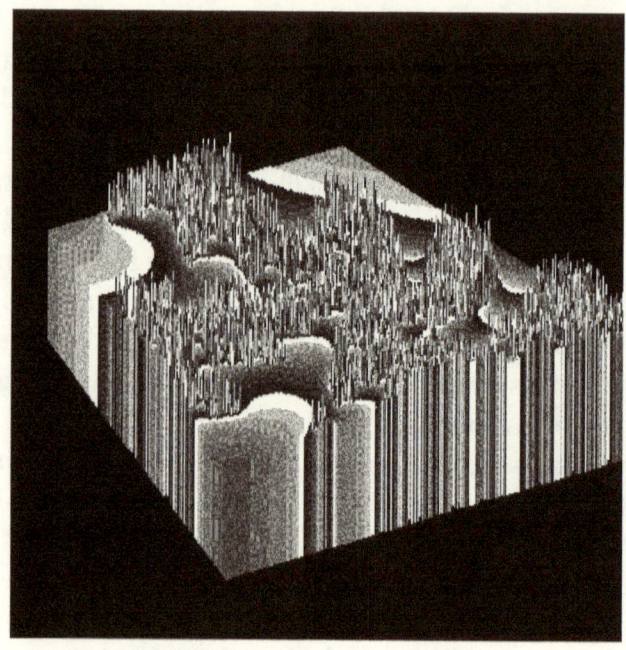

Figure 3-1: A Fitness Landscape

What we are left with at the end of this discussion is that creating and enforcing a vision is no longer a viable strategy. If we have any visual acuity, it is to be able to see the interaction of the system parts at any given time better than others. But to call this ability vision is to totally change the etymology of the word, making a spade a rake instead.

Fitness, Not Vision

Early leaders did not have vision. They made certain that the tribe survived. Survival was a function of fitness. If the leader was physically fit, the tribe was fit and it survived. Maintaining fitness over time required that the tribe adapt to changes in the environment, because the environment would change.

The key to survival of a complex organization is also fitness. *Fitness is defined as behaving in the way that is required of the system at this point in time to enable its survival.*

To understand fitness, consider a landscape as in Figure 3-1. Each peak on the landscape represents one possible solution to a given problem. The highest peak is considered the most fit solution to the problem.

Consider possible mousetrap designs. One peak represents a trap that catches the mouse alive, holding it in a box. Another zaps the poor mouse with an electrical current. A third peak represents a Rube Goldberg type trap, with many connecting contraptions. A fourth is the spring-loaded trap currently (and for many years) in popular use. A peak represents every possible solution.

Fitness is achieved when a satisfactory design is identified and put into practice and the other peaks in sight appear less satisfactory. While searching the fitness space, many alternatives may be tried. As we climb to higher mountains, fewer higher mountains become visible and change in the design becomes incremental, until design changes stop. At that point, you might build a better mousetrap, but you cannot build a fitter one.[42]

Fitness differs from vision in critical ways. First, it is systems oriented. The first historical iteration of vision was inherently systems oriented as well. By being deterministic, the vision outcome was determined by the interaction of the system parts. However, the implied system was linear and, therefore, predictable. There is no assumption of

---

42 For simplicity sake, I have assumed an unchanging landscape. In a later chapter we will look closer at reality when we consider how landscapes change over time and how we can get caught on less then optimum peaks.

an anticipated outcome within the definition of fitness. Therefore, a fitness statement has no values.

Understanding values as vision can involve a systems perspective. The thesis assumes a values-based system, one which operates successfully based upon a predetermined set of behaviors. To succeed, we must assume that there is only one effective value structure for all systems of a certain type (organizational, political, etc.). The goal is to discover that set of values that makes that certain type of system succeed and become aligned with it. This is the presumption of such modern management gurus as Peters.

Of course, if there is only one set of values—one set of processes that will work for that type of system, and every organization follows those values, then the values no longer provide a competitive edge. This results in a state of dynamic equilibrium developing between those companies.

Looking at General Motors at its start, Microsoft, Intel, and other organizations which are succeeding at any given point in time, you will notice that their success frequently comes not from following the rules, but from breaking them. In fact, this rule breaking habit (called symmetry breaking in the scientific literature) is part of the emergent evolutionary process through which we achieve improvements in all endeavors. If the result of breaking a rule is desirable within the system, the rule breaker obtains a short-term advantage over his competitors by breaking the rule. That is because the system's environment has changed. By jumping to a new fitness peak, the rule breaker is the one bringing the system back in line with the needs of the environment.

On our landscape space, rule breaking is like jumping mountains. At a given point in time, all those needing a solution to a problem may have converged on mountain top X. Your company is the first to see a higher peak ahead. As you jump to it, it appears as though you are breaking the rules to all those currently achieving success.

Many people would like to believe that there is some universal set of values that would make everything work well. But in practice, by assuming that one's values are the appropriate values, by practicing those values, one actually disassociates oneself with the continuous change in the larger system, or more immediately, within the organization's immediate environment.

The quantum definition of vision breaks completely free from the notion of systems, of inter-relatedness. The idea that one creates one's own vision implies that the creator is separate from the system, affecting it but not being affected by it. (Remember the thought experiment with the 10 entrepreneurs.)[43] This is the fallacy of the current management paradigm, which attempts to reconcile systems thinking and vision creation. By saying that the fitness is defined by the system. it is placed smack, dab in the middle of a systems perspective. There is no chance for it to break away.

The second difference between fitness and vision is that fitness is concerned with the present time, as opposed to vision's place looking into the future.

Stacey provides the best discussion of the problems associated with such future-oriented planning.[44] First, he recognizes the limitations imposed on the potential for long term planning as a result of the impact of the butterfly effect. More importantly, he sees visioning retreats as a way for organizations to avoid conflict by ignoring important discussions on the current problems being experienced by an organization. Such avoidance only helps organizational members avoid playing the blame game which leads to conflict, rather than enabling the group to address critical issues of the present.

---

43 According to Prigogine, the description that results from such an interpretation is of an atomistic universe, such as that envisioned by the early Greeks. The Greeks were the first to theorize that atoms were the basic constituents of matter. However, rather than recognizing that atoms interact, they pictured them as existing in separate, yet parallel trajectories. We now know that at the atomic and subatomic level, atoms and their components interact consistently and randomly. Ibid.

44 ibid. pps 41–42

Functioning in the present does not mean ignoring the past or failing to be wary of the future. The past always affects the present and the future, whether we like it or not. Chapter 7 presents a case study of how the past impacted Honda's ability to change. The power of the past is the weight of the system's determinism.

But the future is more problematic. Since complex systems are emergent and unpredictable, the future really does not exist until it arrives. Theoretically, then, inclusion of the future should have no place in the planning process. However, it can fit in two ways.

If we again consider the game of pool, a pool shark is able to do short term prediction with relative, but not complete certainty. A system of planning can take into consideration likely, short-term future scenarios. However, the planners must watch the outcomes diligently and be willing to change direction at a moment's notice when the system changes.

For the more long term, while outcomes cannot be predicted with much certainty, boundaries and changes in system behavior can be identified. These forms of prediction are qualitative instead of quantitative. They require the ability to look at patterns of performance over time rather than system outputs either at a given time or over time.

Boundaries are the ultimate potentials of a system. The system's attractor defines them. Chapter 2 discussed the different types of attractors. If over time, a system's outputs do not change, the attractor is a single point attractor, like a pendulum coming to a stop. The system is at equilibrium and there is only one potential outcome. The situation exists when a company which produces, ships, and sells 20 widgets a day, every day, for instance. Because of the immediate boundary, we can predict that if the demand goes up, we will not have the capacity for it. This, in fact, is what happens in the Beer Distribution Game described by Senge. The impact of inserting a simple change in that equilibrium system usually results in the output gyrating out of control.

If an organization finds that sales are high every summer and low every winter and production follows suit, then the system is operating on a limit cycle attractor. Priesmeyer describes this situation for the Toro Company before its adding snow blowers to its product line.[45] From this, we can predict that sales will go up and down during certain periods.

Changing such systems is tricky. Toro tried to move the attractor towards equilibrium by adding snow blowers, thereby evening out sales and production year round. The effect was the opposite. The unexpected change in winter weather created an instability that ran the system into chaos. As with the Beer Distribution Game, making a qualitative change in the system, adding a new component destabilizes the system and even qualitative predictability can be lost.

For complex, multi-product organizations, the variables become more intertwined. What is likely to emerge is a chaotic attractor. Yet there are predictions about behavior that can be made from a chaotic attractor.

The Prediction Company founded by chaoticians Doyne Farmer and Norman Packard and funded by CitiBank, is making predictions on the commodity markets. Their work is based on the discovery of chaotic attractors in the movement of those markets. The company cannot predict specific prices for markets for any given day. But they can predict volatility of direction, including the likelihood that a general trend will continue because of the amount of volatility. They can also predict the boundaries of change. These can be critical predictions for effective investing in commodities.

A likely scenario can also be predicted from each attractor case, so long as one assumes that there will be no change in the attractor. But the attractor is not a trend line into the future. It is a description of what is happening in the present.

The third critical difference between fitness and vision is fitness' reliance on assessing what is required. Visioning makes no such assumption. It is, in essence, narcissistic. Visioning asks, "what do we

---

45 Priesmeyer, ibid.

want our organization to look like in the future?" That was clearly the question asked by the entrepreneur in Jurassic Park.

The idea of requirement can be looked at from different perspectives. In the early 1990's it was popular to think in terms of core competencies. These were the constellation of skills and abilities either existing or desired by an organization, which defined its potential. A company whose core competencies included financial management, customer service, and extensive data processing capability could become a bank, an insurance company, or a brokerage house. But that company cannot become a computer chip manufacturer.

Collaborators insisted that these core competencies represented the organization's attractors because they did help cause the boundaries of performance. This is a misuse of the term attractor, however, because the competencies are not the actual boundaries of performance.

Core competencies do represent another important concept in complex adaptive systems. They are what John Holland calls "tags."[46]

Holland describes tags as a critical component of adaptation in complex systems. He developed the term from the study of genetics. To understand it requires thinking in terms of DNA strands. They are the information codes that make it possible for certain groups to mate while others stay away.

Figure (3-2) shows three strands of DNA material. Consider each one as a separate company. Each strand has 10 genes. The genes are coded to represent different organizational competencies. Let's say that:

M=manufacturing knowledge

F=financial knowledge

S=service skills

E=manufacturing equipment

C=Management information systems

---

46 *Hidden Order: How Adaptation Builds Complexity*

D=Medical abilities
B=Medical equipment

F	C	S	*	*	*	*	*	*	*

M	E	F	*	*	*	*	*	*	*

D	F	C	S	*	*	*	*	*	*

•   ="wildcard", undefined and not critical

Just looking at the three companies, which two would you guess would make the best match? The answer is the top and bottom companies. Why, because they both have a constellation of genes that can be tagged together without disrupting their systems. Company 1 also has the option of adding the one competency to compete with Company 3, possibly by raiding Company 3 if it so desires. But Company 2 is clearly in a league of its own. Any decision to evolve into an organization similar to either of the other two would be catastrophic, similar to trying to mate an ostrich and a canary.

To empirically support this notion, try to determine the actual types of organizations the three companies represent. The first, it turns out, would be a bank. The second would be a manufacturer, the third an insurance company. Clearly, the bank and insurance company have more to gain working together than either one with the manufacturing company.

Tags limit the possible adaptation choices of a system. For the manufacturer to become one of the other companies, it would have to go through a number of intermediate steps to both add and delete some of its genes. Later we will see that this does happen at catastrophic times, particularly when the company has operated too long at equilibrium.

This is a VERY simplified example of how tags work, and it ignores other aspects of emergent adaptation, especially as it is demonstrated with what is known as the genetic algorithm (GA).

Finally, fitness is completely tied up with the notion of survival.

Senge and others suggest that it is critical that the organization not just react, but affect the environment. Within the context of co-evolution, there really is no difference between these two perspectives. When a part of a system reacts to changes elsewhere in the system, it is acting upon the system at the same time. When computer modems were first sold as a commodity, they ran at 300 baud. The market wanted more speed, and various parts of the system had to adjust. Eventually, the modems increased to 12K baud, 24K, 33K baud, and finally 56K baud. You may remember that when the speeds first increased, carriers charged fee differentials based on the speed. That change in the system was rejected quickly. Now, with 56K baud modems available, phone lines and receiving systems do not yet have the bandwidth to handle such lightning speed. So an intermediary step of data compression is included to make the modems function correctly.

The corollary doesn't work, however. If the rest of the system is not ready for your addition, it will not accept it. If you are on the highest peak already, stepping off will lead to a fall. As we saw, just building a better mousetrap will not result in selling your new mousetrap, as thousands of inventors learned. When Ford tried to sell the Edsel, it experienced the same reaction. Effective action and reaction turn out to be the flip sides of the same coin.

If there is any "vision" in complex systems, it is survival. However, it is not always clear what is meant to survive. Is the organization as a whole the unit of survival?

Traditionally, if a market changes significantly, an organization is expected to collapse. The less complex the organization, the more likely smaller environmental changes can lead to collapse. Single product entrepreneurial companies are a good example.

More complex organizations are more diversified, they roam across more fitness landscapes. It is the diversity that allows them to weather system changes, so long as they are positioned to adapt. However, even these companies collapse, which is one of the reasons why the average life of even institutionalized companies is only 50 years. The reason for the collapse is tied all to often to emphasis on vision and direction, rather than fitness.

Discovering Fitness

The fitness of a newly established organization is dependent upon whether the founders have understood their product or service correctly relative to the environment. If the founders have developed a new product that will create a new market, then fitness will be dependent upon the readiness of the market to accept the product. The founder can also expect competition from numerous competitors with potentially similar design solutions. These are all experiments which will later travel the trail towards the fitness peak upon which only a few can live.

More often, a new company will fall onto a fitness peak, frequently one which is not the same as originally intended. When organized, the company is actually searching across the fitness landscape till it finds a peak upon which to rest.

Metritech was originally established by its founder, Sam Krug, to develop, publish, and market high quality computer-based personality tests. The company opened with a couple of tests ready to go. One was a traditional personality test that could be used for psychological evaluation and employee selection. The second was an organizational culture test.

The latter test and Krug's contacts in education enabled him to develop a program for assessing and training school principals. That led to further education-based contracts leading to a major contract to develop school achievement tests. While these latter tests were computer scored, the large numbers involved and the need for continued research led to this one service becoming a major portion of the company's business. The function, or "core business" of the company had significantly changed along its path towards fitness, although the tags remained relatively constant.

Apple Computers demonstrates the potential pitfalls of this process. When Apple's first computer was available for market, the company rightfully believed that the greatest market was first for hobbyists, and then for educators. Pursuing these markets placed it onto a moderately high fitness peak. From its vantagepoint, it was difficult for the company to see the potential for business applications. As a result, it failed to take a step to the next higher peak quickly enough to take advantage of the expanded market. Meanwhile, a large number of manufacturers led by IBM experimented with Intel processors, Microsoft's DOS operating system, and their own business software applications. These companies scurried around the fitness landscape until reaching a higher peak than Apple. By the time Apple entered the business market, the environment DOS was the foundation for the new peak. Although Apple had the technically better operating system and faster processing time, others reading the changing landscape had outflanked it.

Eventually, a shared fitness peak is reached until only a large change— a system bifurcation, can open up new opportunities. Currently it appears as though Apple's only choice to survive is to jump onto the Intel-Microsoft (WinTel) fitness peak. Its failure to do so would constitute the same stubbornness demonstrated by those early flyers who insisted on airplanes with multiple wings.

Arie de Geus describes excellent examples of how long living companies like Royal Dutch Shell even change their core businesses over time in order to be able to survive.[47] While this is not the only method for organizational survival in a complex world, it is the one least considered

---

47 de Geus, Arie. *The Living Organization*

by those who feel that the key to their future is through continued refinement of an existing product or product line.

By the way, nonprofit organizations are notorious for following similar random walks over changing fitness landscapes. Over time, their core businesses are forced to change in response to the changing whims of funders and changes in the needs of clientele. Changes in party control of local, state, and national politics can whipsaw a nonprofit into oblivion if it fails to quickly adapt. Constant change is the only way to maintain fitness in the nonprofit world.

Conclusion

An organization can easily become less than fit for their environment.

At the time this chapter was written, F.W. Woolworth had just decided to close its Five and Ten Cents Stores that had been around for 177 years. The company recognized that product mix, the automobile, geographical location of existing stores, shopping habits, and competition from mega-stores had all taken their toll on this uniquely American institution. (Interestingly, they are not closing their stores in Germany and Mexico.) The company recognized that the fitness landscape had changed so much that these stores could not catch up.

But the company had been adapting all along. In place of the Five and Tens, Woolworth's will site some of their smaller, boutique-like stores such as The Locker Room. The institution of the Five and Ten Cents Store may be gone, but by adapting, the company lives on. The only question remains, could the institution, itself, have evolved into one that would have competed with the Wal-Marts and Super K-Marts? The answer, sometimes yes, sometimes no.

Chapter 4

Holsight: Looking for Fitness

Alice is lost at a fork in the woods. Out pops the Cheshire Cat on a tree limb. Alice asks: "Kindly Mr. Cheshire cat, could you tell me which way I ought to go?" "Well, that depends upon where you'd like to be," responds to toothy feline. "Well, I really don't know," says Alice. "Then it really doesn't matter," says the Cat.

For a long time, the story of Alice and the Cheshire Cat has served as a metaphor for strategic planning: It reflected the belief that planning and change involved knowing where one is and where one wants to be. Strategy was a matter of plotting the straightest route from here to there.

But the formula breaks down when the future is not visible. Today, the scenery changes too fast. All that we have is where we are right now. In a complex Wonderland, the Cheshire's question should be, "Well that depends on where you are right now? Alice never knew the answer to this question, either.

Organizations like to believe that they do know where they are, yet much more time is spent worrying about the future and building in controls to reach it. Stacey demonstrates that this future-oriented approach is used to avoid the conflicts that erupt when stakeholders try to share their perceptions of the present.[48]

In the linear world of the industrial revolution, it was possible to plot the path from point A to point B. From knowing one's position and direction, it was easy to predict what would be ahead in the woods. Being just a little off made little difference, because the outcome would also be only a little off the track.

Progress on the path was measured by comparing outputs—the number of widgets made and sold, the percent of market share enabling this, the profits realized from these activities—against the markers in the plan. Variation was quickly corrected, the team was pushed back on course to the planned direction.

Managers know intuitively that unpredictability affects the plan. They fight about it each year during the annual performance evaluation, when they are forced to justify why the plan was not achieved. Process can be understood, past performance can be measured. However, this, too, provides little help in planning direction. It is like driving while all the time looking out through the rear view mirror.

Management today requires driving through unexplored territory. With an ever-changing fitness landscape, road maps don't exist. Only a compass can help. I call the ability to navigate through this territory, *holsight.*

Holsight is the ability to systemically look at one's situation in the here and now to determine what fits and what needs to be changed in order to survive.

Holsight provides insight into the fitness of an organization by exposing connections and patterns that are ignored in traditional organizational analysis. It starts by observing behavior over time, by watching the organization as a movie or video instead of as a series of snap

---

48 Ibid. Stacey

shots. Observing changes over time exposes relationships, which lead to a system understanding of the behavior. These patterns are not truly causal, either because the number of variables involved overwhelms the ability to fault one input, or because the time distance between cause and effect are two far to be traced. That is why emphasis is placed on the behavior of the whole system, rather than its parts. Hence, *hol*sight.

The most controversial part of this definition is the emphasis on survival. Is that the true responsibility of an organization? Managers tend to reject this thesis "No!", they cry. "Organizations exist to serve their customers, or to provide employment to their workers, or to increase the capacity of the society. If they can't do these things, they will not be able to compete and should be allowed to die" states popular opinion.

de Geus provides a compelling argument in support of survival as the prime objective. He distinguishes between two kinds of organizations. de Geus describes the *economic organization* as one whose purpose is to make money for the owners. Economic organizations are short lived, as de Geus shows in his book. de Geus's second type of organization is the *living company*. He writes about this organizational style: "Like all organisms, the living company exists primarily for its survival and improvement: to fulfill its potential and to become as great as it can be."[49]

Survival is easily defined and measured. But how do we define potential or greatness? Is it a function of size, of community and human potential (as de Geus seems to think), of product quality? In a complex world, these descriptions of greatness can conflict with the need to survive. Sometimes just hanging in there is more than enough.

Fitness replaces greatness. The switch establishes that *organizations exist primarily for their own survival, which they achieve by maintaining an appropriate degree of fitness with their environment.*

---

49 de Geus, Arie, *The Living Company*, p 11

One could argue that fitness and greatness are the same things. Were a given fitness landscape a static entity, this would be true. As proposed in social Darwinism, the fittest are at the top of the highest peak.

However, fitness landscapes, themselves, change over time. Planned and unplanned changes in the environment lead to externally driven and collaterally driven co-evolution. A high peak one year may be just an average peak the next year. Paying extra to be on the highest peak one day (such as purchasing the hottest 8-track tape player), may maroon you on the peak later on.

Most likely, greatness will take a company beyond adaptability. Beta was a great video recording system, VHS was a good one. Apple MacIntosh was a great computer, DOS based IBMs were good ones, dinosaurs were great animals, the smaller, dog like animals that eventually evolved into humans were just good ones. As many companies have learned instinctively, when the issue is survival, good is good enough as long as the company maintains its eye on the fitness landscape.

Purpose and Holsight

There has been extensive discussion over the years between whether organizations should "stick to the knitting" by defining very specific visions and mission, or whether they should create broad visions to allow for adaptation over time. On the one hand, research into entrepreneurial organizations has supported Peters' claim that when the organization strays too far from its original intentions, it loses touch with its customers as its vision and its image becomes muddled. This led many companies to spin-off successful (and unsuccessful) ventures, and to hold business units down to 500 or less employees. Peters' current call to destruction is the ultimate cry of this claim. [50]

---

50 Peters, Tom, *In Search of Excellence, and Circle of Innovation*

Others have pressed for broad visions to allow organizations to adjust and adapt as technologies change. These studies point to the destruction of the great railroads, typewriter companies, and other technology-driven companies because their confined missions forbade them from adapting.

Emphasizing fitness is a way out of this paradox. Fitness allows the organization to address whatever is necessary for survival. What it does at any given point in time is the organization's purpose.

Purpose defines what an organization does right now to survive. For instance, the original purpose of 3M was to make sandpaper. Now the company can be considered multipurpose. Or its purpose can be defined by the constellation of resources that it uses to produce the products that it sells. This might read something like, "We make products which involve the use of adhesive materials."

With fitness paramount, purpose is changeable. A company can totally switch products and/or technologies if such is needed to survive, without first checking the mission statement.

This, in fact, is what Penn Central Corporation has done to survive. Penn Central started as the Pennsylvania Railroad in 1847. In 1968, it merged with two other East Coast railroads to become the Penn Central Corporation. During the first two years, the corporation began to diversify into financial industries. Those who support the notion of "sticking to the knitting" suggest that this diversification was the cause of Penn Central's bankruptcy in 1970. From this book's perception, it was the corporation's salvation.

Penn Central is still around today. The company operated as a railroad until 1975, when Conrail took over its rail assets. Then it continued as a financial company, specializing in insurance, a key acquisition from its diversification. In 1995, the company changed its name to

American Premier Underwriters and, as of this writing, is solvent and involved in further mergers.[51]

Unfortunately, we do not know what thinking went on in Penn Central's boardroom at the time of the acquisition binge. In retrospect, one hopes that the Board recognized the downturn in the rail industry, hoped for a takeover-bailout by government, and began its diversification as a strategy for survival. If it did, then the Board exhibited holsight.

de Geus points out that the 30 long lived organizations that his group at Dutch/Shell Oil Company studied all demonstrated changes in their core business—their purpose—over time. Although those changes were not easy, they did enable one company to survive over 600 years!

If survival is the primary need of an organization, then the organization must have the option of changing its core business or purpose. The problem is whether the organization has a built in capacity to effectively allow such change to emerge naturally, because, as discussed in Chapter 5, it is not likely to happen when planned.

The notion of changing the purpose represents a major hurdle to the ego-driven nature of entrepreneurial organizations. Organizations like Apple Computers, Digital Equipment Corporation, Wolfram Research, Wang, etc, are built on turning the founder's innovation into an ongoing enterprise. Each entrepreneur believes that his or her product is the best and should, with enough capital and competitive marketing, beat the competition out of the market. If the fitness landscape stayed static and if the entrepreneur's invention stood on the highest fitness peak, then this would be true.

But the invention and competitiveness of others changes the relationship of these peaks. The competition is also attempting to find the best fitness, morphing the fitness landscape to the point when the product and/or technology will converge towards one new peak. Only a few

---

51 From *The Penn Central Railroad Home Page http://prozac.cwru.edu/jer/pc/pc_nf.html*

can survive on each peak. When that time comes, the others will need to adapt to different environments or merge into a successful company to provide continuation of the relationships that have built up in the entrepreneur's organization.

Holsight allows organizations to read and navigate through the ever-changing fitness landscape. In some ways it is easier for leaders in large diversified companies like Penn Central, because their companies have already passed through the dangerous white water of single product survival. Their boats can be like rubber rafts, their diversity provides the cushioning that allows them to bounce off the rocks of change. For the entrepreneur, the boat is a kayak. Kayaks have the ability to punch a hole in their competitor's raft. But for the majority of entrepreneurs, an unseen rock will smash their organizations to bits.

Holsight as Qualitative Analysis

Quantitative analysis is numbers crunching. It is accounting, statistical analysis, additive in nature. Quantitative analysis stresses inputs and outputs, actual against plan, benchmarking, establishing and meeting expectations.

Qualitative analysis is no less rigorous than quantitative analysis. (Nor should it replace quantitative analysis.) But qualitative analysis emphasizes process and the behavior of the system. Although this can be deduced from the outputs, there are other points of information that can also come into play.

Science historian Stephen Kellert describes how science itself is changing its emphasis to qualitative analysis from quantitative analysis as a result of the emerging new science. *"As a qualitative study, chaos theory investigates a system by asking about the general character of its long-term behavior, rather than seeking to arrive at numerical predictions about its exact future state,"* explains Kellert[52]. Gleick makes much of the same distinction when he describes the new science as a science of process [53]

What does it look like to analyze process? A quantitative analysis may compare a company's stock price on a given day for each of the last three years. Over the past year the price went up 3 percentage points. The previous year it went up 2 percentage points. We can also say that there was a 5% increase in the value of the stock over the past 3 years.

It would be difficult, but do-able, to do a qualitative analysis of the same information. Generally, more data points would be needed. For instance, you might consider the daily close of the stock. As a result, the qualitative analysis might read: "Over the past three years, there has been a continuous increase in the rate of growth of the stock value. At the same time, the stock has increased in volatility, with greater differences between the highs and lows.

This qualitative analysis tells us something more than just the quantitative information usually supplied in annual reports. In fact, qualitative analysis may demonstrate that it was by pure chance that the stock was up on the anniversary date, making the increase transparent and a false indicator of organizational health.

Attempts to understand the behavior of the US Stock Market during the last half of 1997 further demonstrates the importance of qualitative analysis. The difference between the Dow Jones Industrial Index value at market close on June 1, 1997 and December 31, 1997 was 250 points. The market changed 3 percent during those six months. Given the luxury of choosing a stopping point 3 days earlier, the result would have shown a flat market for the six months. If a fund manager relies only

---

52 Kellert, Stephen H. *In the Wake of Chaos* ppgs 3-4
53 Gleick, James. *Chaos: The making of a new science*

this information to plan for the future, s/he would assume a very quiet market, similar to the pre-1980s stock market.

The analysis also masks the fact that in August, the market hit its all time high, and in October, had its worst one-day point loss ever. More importantly, the analysis would miss demonstrating how volatile the market was throughout this period.

During the past two decades, a number of new, qualitative strategies have been developed to analyze the stock market. Public interest has centered on complicated market timing strategies. Strategies coming from the new sciences include the use of neural networks to identify market patterns, and Deere & Company's use of genetic algorithms to plan investment strategies.[54] These methods surpass the traditional market view as rising, falling, or volatile—waiting to make a decision.

Another approach is based on the concept of self-organized critical-ity. Most economists consider the last half of 1997 as a period of high market volatility. But an alternate review of the market's behavior sug-gests that it reached a limit to its growth. That raises the first question—what caused the limit to be reached? The answer: a period of self-organized criticality.

Per Bak and Kan Chen identified the concept of self-organized criti-cality by dropping sand onto a pile, one-grain at a time. In their experi-ments, they discovered that when a certain diameter is reached for the coned pile, the pile starts having periodic avalanches. Some are small, some large, and the size of any particular one cannot be predicted. Yet, the size relationship of each to the others is predictable.[55] The pile reaches this point when the diameter of the pile's base can no longer

---

54 The Genetic Algorithm is one form of self-organization that follows the developmental process described in Chapter 6. Neural networks will be explained in Chapter 7 as part of the discussion on learning organisms.

55 Bak, Per and Chen, Kan, "Self-Organized Criticality." *Scientific American*, January, 1991, 46–54

support the weight of the pile. The avalanches enable the pile to create a larger base, unless the perimeter of the pile's table has been reached.

If self-organized criticality has developed, then the fund manager should act differently than acting as though the fund is rising, falling, or waiting to make a decision. S/he should invest based on the assumption that the bull market is over for the moment, but that the periodic catastrophes will not set off a bear market. On any given day, the market will rise or fall unpredictably any given amount, regardless of what's happening in other news stories. Under the circumstances, value investing should probably replace growth investing for the long term, until the overall base of investment increases to be able to support a higher market.

Time and Holsight

One of the critical shifts in thinking necessary for a nonlinear systems perspective is to view performance flowing over time, instead of at discrete points in time. Traditional management indicators, like quarterly reports, turnover ratios, P/E ratios, current stock price, error rates, sales price, etc. are used as snapshots that freeze time. They ignore important information about system changes over time, and so have less meaning for understanding a complex system.

A cornerstone of complex systems analysis is time series analysis—the change in performance over time—in one form or another. Instead of a snapshot, effective time series analysis is like a three dimensional video.

The stock market example above showed how a stock's value on any given day is unpredictable. So is sales revenue, inventory, production output, absenteeism, etc. Relying on discrete observations of changes in stock value on set days is a dangerously inaccurate method of analysis when times are turbulent.

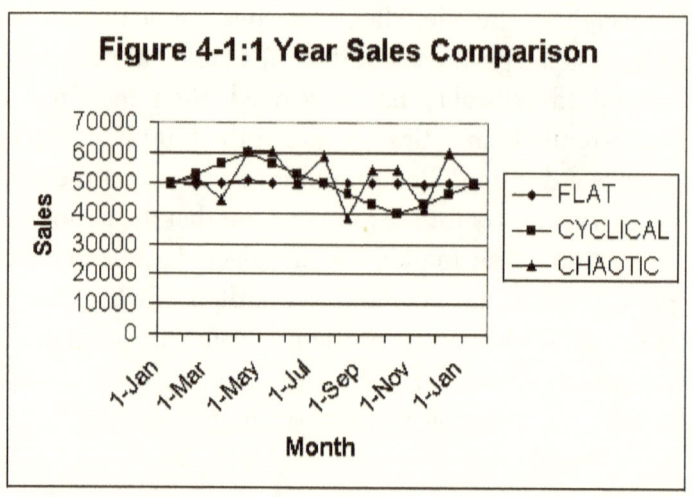

Figure 4-1:1 Year Sales Comparison

Consider evaluating daily sales revenues. The three lines on Figure 4-1 represent fictitious sales revenues during a three-year period. For each year, the revenue is the same on the first and last day of the year. Ignoring the information in the middle leads to the assumption that each year was comparable. The difference only shows up looking between the discrete points in time.

Looking between the points, Line 1 shows a very stable year. While such an outcome as a straight line is rare for daily sales revenues, when there is very little fluctuation, sales will be considered "flat" for the year. For this year the original analysis of a flat year holds true.

Line 2 shows sales increasing and decreasing, but the extent of increase and decrease is always the same. Total sales revenue for the year will turn out to be flat, since the valleys neutralize the peaks.

It is wrong treat the year as flat in this scenario. The sales were cyclical. It takes a different management strategy to cope with cycles than to cope with a flat line. The manager will need to question the causes of the cycle, whether the cycle could and should be broken, and if not broken, how to insure timely supplies to decrease inventory and maximize revenues. Cash flow then becomes another headache for this manager.

Line 3 also shows the sales revenues to be almost the same at the beginning and end of the year. But in between, what a mess, like the second half of 1997's stock market! There is no pattern, only chaos. Certainly, knowing the behavior of sales revenues under this circumstance is critical in order to survive. Not only do we ask what is causing the pattern, but how do we survive with the pattern if necessary? Interestingly enough, in this case the valleys and peaks may not neutralize each other. This could be a year of increased or decreased total sales!

Visually inspecting a time series analysis provides considerable information. There are a number of strategies for more in-depth analysis of time series. [56] By now, you should recognize the three graphs as the same as those used for explaining the logistics equation in Chapter 2. They are also symptomatic of the changeability of a system, as will be described in the next chapter. This recognition opens management to analyses strategies such as Priesmeyer's. Priesmeyer developed an analysis based on the metaphor of a heartbeat. To Priesmeyer, time series analysis is like looking at the results of an electrocardiogram. A simple review of two or three indicators can explain whether a company is experiencing an arrhythmia, a heart attack requiring quick action, or normal behavior. [57]

The Systemic Nature of Holsight

Chapter 2 provided an overview of systems thinking. To reiterate, the purpose of systems thinking is to try to identify the relationships

---

56 See The Fifth Discipline *Feildbook* by Peter Senge and others, for a good introduction to converting time series data to systems concepts in its section on Systems Thinking. This book's goal is to add tools from complexity theory to the work already done.

57 Priesmeyer, Ibid.

between parts of the system that result in the currently observed behavior of the system.

Two related forms of systems analysis have arisen in the past 30 years. System dynamics is a method for establishing a theoretical model of the feedback relationships in a nonlinear system, identify or estimate mathematical relationships between those parts, manipulate the variables by trying different inputs in the mathematical formulas, and observe the system's behavior under these varying conditions. Almost any type of system can be modeled, although software that has been developed for this purpose is still a little clumsy[58]

System dynamics allows the manager to test options and observe likely behavioral results based on the alternatives chosen. System dynamics shows what's happening in the system under a given set of constructs.

Dynamical systems analysis is a part of complex systems theory. Dynamical systems analysis helps the observer see emergent behavior of a system over time. The analysis converts time series data into a graphical image that identifies the potential and boundaries of the system.

A critical difference is that the dynamical analysis has shifted from a one dimensional graphics representation to a multi-dimensional representation of the outputs. There are three dimensions in the dynamical analysis, representing 3 variables, X, Y and time. The graph is created in phase space (or state space diagram), called such because it shows that state of each of the variables within the system at each point in time. A phase diagram can have any number of dimensions, depending upon the number of variables being considered in the system.

---

58 Stella for Macintosh and VenSim for Windows and DOS are two very popular software packages for system dynamics modeling. See also *The Fifth Discipline Fieldbook* for an overview of the process of systems modeling.

Holsight as Pattern Recognition

One of the greatest contributions of complexity theory has been its emphasis on pattern recognition as a basis for qualitative analysis. Pattern creation and recognition is also at the core of the learning process. It is how the brain operates to identify information coming into in.

Two types of patterns are discussed in the new science: emergent patterns and self-similar patterns. Emergent patterns show the behavior of a system, emphasizing the boundaries and potential of the system. This provides options for decision making. Self-similar patterns make it possible to apply what is known about behavior in one context to another situation.

The last section showed three lines on a typical X/Y graph. The X-axis represented time, the Y axis represented output at each point in time. The graph should look familiar to you. It is the same as those in Chapter 2 describing the logistics equation.

Figures 2-8, 2-9, and 2-6 in Chapter 2 are the phase space diagrams associated with those graphs. But in this case, the X-axis represents **change** in sales revenues, instead of actual revenues, from each point to the next. (Point 1, for instance, would be Day 2 sales minus Day 1 sales; point 2 would be Day 3 sales minus Day 2 sales; etc.)

Figure 2-8 shows the "flat" sales as a single point attractor. We interpret such attractors as meaning that the system goes towards equilibrium. Looking at the original X/Y graph, the fact that the system reaches a single point makes sense. On the X/Y graph, the outputs reach a certain level and remain at that level. There is no change.

For many reasons, equilibrium feels like the best place for any manager to be. Everything is running smoothly, so the manager can go out and play tennis without worrying. While that turns out to be a false assumption when the rest of the world is crazy, it does establish that no change is happening, so plan accordingly.

Figure 2-9, describing the behavior of the second line, demonstrates a limit cycle attractor. This system is held together by the two points. (Limit cycle attractors can have more than two points, but the line will always end up following the same path.) Such a limit cycle could be the result of a company selling a seasonal item, for instance. Many small consulting firms operate under limit cycles because when the principals are working, they do not have time to market and when they are marketing, there is no income from chargeable time.

Figure 2-6 shows the system as a chaotic attractor. The surprise in chaotic attractors is that the erratic behavior of the third line on the X/Y graph produces a bounded figure in phase space. However, the system never returns to the same exact position twice. If it did, it would repeat the cycle and be a limit cycle attractor.

The condition of the third example is a system that is always changing. It develops in systems where the independent variables are too numerous or intertwined to be controlled.

For instance, let's say that the number of nail suppliers has been reduced to 3 over the years. A new company enters the market introducing a new product, liquid nails. No more hammering, no more smashed fingers, no more holes in walls. The landscape has been upset and the search is on for a new type of fitness. Such a condition can produce a chaotic attractor such as this.[59]

On first blush, managers fear this chaos. The path is unpredictable. But leaders will need to learn to embrace the chaotic attractor whenever their organizations are traveling through white water rapids.

Three dynamics of a chaotic attractor enable the system to continue to function. First, the attractor defines the potential boundaries of behavior for the system. If all the spaces in phase space were visited,

---

[59] Sometimes I wonder if the relationship between screws with Phillips heads and traditional screws breaks this pattern, because I could never understand the need for Phillips head screws!

then there would be true and complete randomness. This condition would be unmanageable. Remember, the chaotic attractor associated with the global weather system assures us that it will not snow in Miami FL in July or be 100 degrees in Miami OH in January, because these two points of potential behavior do not lie on the attractor.

Secondly, the attractor exhibits self-similarity at different levels. This means that there will be periods of time when events within the system will appear more stable. There will be breathing spaces.

Most importantly, there are more options available to the system when the edge of chaos is reached. As the scientist Mitchell Feigenbaum once stated, "at the edge of chaos, all is possible."[60] Adaptation becomes possible at the edge of chaos because there is a greater diversity of potential than when the system is operating on either of the other two attractors.

You probably realize by now that all three outcomes developed from the same system model, the logistics equation. The variable distinguishing between them is the amount of input, often discussed in terms of energy that is pushed into the system. The higher the energy, the more likely the system will experience the limit cycle or chaotic attractor condition.

There is a very famous population dynamics exercise that follows these patterns, and can be modeled on system dynamics software. Called the "Predator-Prey Model," it tracks the population dynamics between foxes and rabbits (or two other animals of which one feeds on the other) in a given ecological niche.

At the lowest level, if there are not enough foxes or not enough Rabbits, the system will come to equilibrium—both species will die. Why? The three variables are the foxes, the rabbits, and the amount of grass in the niche for the rabbits to feed on. When there are too few foxes, the rabbits keep reproducing until there are more rabbits than available grass, they eat all the grass, and then perish. If there are too

60 From an address by Mitchell Feigenbaum made at Nobel Conference XXVI, Gustavus Adolphus College, St Peters MN, Oct 2, 1990.

many foxes, they eat all the rabbits, then have no food, and they also die of starvation. In system dynamics, by the way, this is primary archetypal system created through a reinforcing feedback loop.

There is a range in which the system moves into a limit cycle. With enough rabbits, foxes, and grass, a symbiotic relationship develops. As the number of foxes increase, the number of rabbits decrease to a point where there are not enough rabbits to sustain the foxes. The number of foxes decrease, allowing more rabbits to be born and live to reproduction age, thereby increasing their population. Once the rabbit population is large enough, more foxes can live. The cycle repeats itself. This is the limit to growth archetype in system dynamics language.

Finally, if you add a second predator, or make some other variation, the system changes to the chaotic attractor.

This is just one of many pattern-creating models that show up in our social systems. I've chosen it to demonstrate pattern recognition because of its direct correlation to a real business problem, the history of the airline industry.

Consider the changes in the airline industry over time. Before deregulation, the industry experienced stability—equilibrium. The number of airlines in the US remained relatively constant: Pan Am, TWA, Delta, American and Eastern were the big ones, with a few regional companies like Allegheny Airlines (now US Airways). Prices also remained stable relative to inflation. There was equilibrium.

Following deregulation, the system bifurcated into a new pattern that matches the Predator-Prey Model's limit cycle. After deregulation, new companies joined the market with lower prices. This caused the major carriers to lower their prices to compete. Some of the major carriers (Eastern for instance) and some of the new carriers (i.e. Midway) could not last, since the amount of resources (revenues) could not sustain the larger numbers of seats. After this period of retrenchment, prices rose again. Again, new carriers came in with lower prices. The existing carriers had to lower their prices. Again, some could not compete and either folded or merged.(i.e. Pan Am) Once the number of carriers were down again, prices started to rise, again. We are now at the point where new carriers are slowly beginning to come into the market to offset rising prices.

Recognizing the pattern opens a new set of options for survival. The traditional approach would be to fight at all times for market share with the lowest cost highest revenue strategy. An alternative strategy in this case is to ask what phase of the cycle the company is in and determine how to respond based on that phase. Number 1 in market share during the price cutting phase may provide the most dangerous option, since it could require deep cuts which put the company's finances at risk. Once again, just being good may be good enough.

What could drive this system into the chaotic regime? The development of a new mode of transportation that re-sculptured the fitness landscape. As we have seen with the development of supersonic flight, not every new introduction will take the system to the point of chaos. And it is not easy to predict which changes will take the system to the edge of chaos. That lack of knowledge is another one of the uncertainties of complex systems. However, if the system does go into chaos, the response needed to survive will be totally different than the ones used to survive the cycles.

Foxes and rabbits like the airline industry? One of the infinite cases of self-similarity that enables an organization to learn through a cross-disciplinary approach to problem-solving.

Besides this vertical example, self-similarity can also be horizontal. Behavior at one level of an organization can also prove similar to behavior at a higher or lower level.

The Beer Distribution Game described previously demonstrates that self-similarity can also emerge in the outcomes of the organization's efforts. Performance is evaluated over time with graphs of on-hand inventory. This results in graphs with similar peaks and valleys whose appearance is different only in the intensity of each peak and the time it was reached. Similarly, waves of high production and boondoggles are likely to move through a production facility, rather than just showing up in one place.

Vertical self-similarity, sometimes called fractal relationships, are most prominent in studies of organizational cultures. For instance, organizations demonstrate similar team styles throughout an organization. If, for instance, the executive team operates like a baseball team (a lot of individualistic star players), then similar team behavior is found elsewhere in the organization. Robert Golembiewski has found that stress reaction will also be duplicated at different levels of an organization.

Organizational structures can also repeat themselves through different levels of a company. Clearly a defined correlation exists between the main office structure in a school system, the administrative structure of different schools in the system, and the organizing of the classroom itself. The vector that brings about such alignment can be as simple as the structure of the administrative (paperwork) flow within the district.

Vertical self-similarity is a form of alignment. Elsewhere in this book, I have argued against trying to create an alignment of vision, values, or culture in an organization, demonstrating how such an alignment can hinder the ability to adapt and survive.

However, it may be that naturally evolved self-similar structures provide a substitute type of organizational alignment. Self-similarity appears to create vectors through which change can pass more easily over time. This would create a feeling of flow regarding change in an organizational setting that would make for a more natural process of change over time.

Conclusion

The purpose of this chapter has been to introduce you to the idea that qualitative analysis is a key component for finding your way when exploring uncharted domains. Our brains are already hard wired to do some pattern recognition. In fact, many discoveries start with intuiting that a pattern exists and then working to prove that it really is there.

This chapter has used self-organized criticality, the logistics equation, and self-similarity as three possible complex systems models for evaluating organizational behavior. But consider this only a sample. True, the models appear to apply to a number of cases. However, the most effective way to understand patterns and relationships is to start the analysis from scratch. Software exists, and will become more prevalent for using raw data to identify attractors and other patterns of behavior of a specific system.

On the other hand, don't fool yourself into believing that you create the patterns on the landscape. Once two people try to create their own patterns, the patterns interfere with each other. They will create uncharted territory that neither competitor will, at first, understand. That is the nature of reinforcing feedback—co-evolution.

At the same time, expect to see tools develop to help with pattern recognition in complex situations. System dynamics software has already been described. Elsewhere, I talked about neural networks and genetic algorithms. These, too are pattern recognition programs. Graphical experiences such as micro-worlds and simulations like Sim-City will provide the opportunity to test out explorations before undertaking real steps. Specialists will also emerge to do the grunt work.

These new tools will show up at all levels of organization. The Prediction Company experiments with commodities trading using their understanding of chaotic attractors. Richard Morley's companies have applied aspects of self-organizing systems to scheduling the Bullet Train and to production floor control at General Motors and elsewhere.

We are just now entering the Forrest in our exploration of new strategies for analysis and planning.

Chapter 5

Changing Change to Maintain Fitness

Draw a boat representing your organization—just the boat, not the water.

Often, people will draw employees crying for help or falling out of their boats. Sometimes the boats will be elaborate, like a three mast tall ship. Other times it is just a row boat with one person in it. Some have holes in them. There have been a few submarines. Nevertheless, over 90 percent draw some kind of hard-hulled boat.

Boats are frequently used as metaphors for organizations. Many organizations actually use the "ship" metaphor as part of their vision. Insurance companies, brokerage firms, and consulting firms discuss securely captaining your assets through risky waters.

Our management artists usually describe their organizations as having hard hulls because traditional management theory expects the steel or wood to provide protection from the buffeting waves on the high seas. The shape and weight provide more stability to steer in the direction of the next port, to steer towards the vision.

The hulls of organizations are built from overlapping control systems. These are the balancing feedback loops which act like gyroscopes to keep the boat upright and on course in calmer waters.

At about the same time as Gleick published his groundbreaking book on chaos theory,[61] Peter Vaill established the term, "permanent white water" as a central focus of management literature.[62] Vaill quoted a participant in one of his workshops who claimed that his organization's environment was like being on a permanent white water river. Things changed in this participant's world so quickly that just holding on took all his effort.

In our world, more and more activity is being squeezed into the area of the Universe called Earth. Two hundred fifty years ago, it could take weeks for a message to get from company headquarters in London to the domestic office in Boston. Now, that message can travel down a river of fiber optic cable at the speed of light. Two hundred and fifty years ago it could take two days to travel from one town to the next. Today it takes a few hours to go across continents, with the holdup being the delay at the airport. Two hundred and fifty years ago we lived in cities of only a few thousand people. Today we may squeeze two million people into the same square acreage. Relative to our ancestors' experience, our environment has become like a permanent white water river. Have we figured out yet how to adapt to the new environment?

A river becomes dangerous when there is more water in the river from heavy rains, when the capacity of the river is reduced at a shallow spot, or the angle of descent increases. The molecules of water move around freely and slowly when the river is deep, the slope shallow, and the width wide. Change any one of the variables and the molecules begin to bounce against each other more frequently, resulting in turbulence.

Take a second to draw the turbulent white water river under your boat. Make sure there are waves, rocks, eddies, sharp turns and steep descents! What do you think will happen to your hard-hulled boat in

---

61 Gleick, ibid.
62 Vaill, Peter. *Managing as a Performing Art*

this new environment. As white water rafters always explain, it will crash on the rocks and sink!

What does succeed is a more flexible boat—a rubber raft. Kayaks also work, but they take more energy and cunning to survive, a mistake in a kayak is more treacherous.

The relationship between the river and the boat provides a good metaphor to evaluate an organization's ability to change and adapt. The build up of the flow from stand still to turbulent matches the movement of systems from equilibrium to chaos.

White water rafters think of rivers in terms of six classes of turbulence, from a Class 1 calm river to a raging Class 6 ride like on portions of the Colorado River. For the purpose of illustration, I will refer to only three of these classes to help explain the process of change. Eventually we will observe what happens in a raging white water river and why the flexibility of the rubber raft provides the greatest chance to get through.

Class 1 Rivers and Equilibrium Organizations

A Class 1 river runs slow. There are occasional rapids with low regular waves. The course is easily determined and there are rescue spots along the way. The boat might sit dead in the water if the occupants do not row. The boat is at equilibrium.

At first glance, equilibrium appears idyllic. There is no change. Everything is under the control of the managers, who see a close relationship between the planned and actual course. So managers intuitively seek this condition.

Chapter 4 described the predator-prey systems model. In the case where there were too many rabbits or too many foxes, both rabbits and foxes eventually died. The system went to a single, unchanging point. It was at equilibrium.

The single point attractor graphically defines a system at equilibrium. A system's behavior has energy at the start, but it eventually winds down and comes to a standstill. The phase space diagram shows the line leading to a single point and staying there.

There is no energy in a system at equilibrium. For a boat to move down river under these conditions, the rowers must supply energy. In calm waters, managers, acting as boatswains, can be in complete charge of the direction of the system.

Traditional controls hold an organization at equilibrium. These include budgets, quality inspections, and performance management systems. They are designed to keep an organization on a pre-planned course. Such controls act as balancing feedback systems. The plans establish the direction of attack for the rowers, and the performance management systems insure that the direction is maintained.

So long as its environment appears to be functioning at equilibrium and the occupants keep rowing, equilibrium is not a problem. The organization may not realize that it is at equilibrium, however. Internally, change appears to happen. But the balancing feedback insures that changes, such as new personnel, do not affect the output, the direction of the boat. In other words, the balancing feedback dampens the potential impact of change.

Equilibrium organizations define the type of organizations and their environments that existed prior to the industrial revolution. Change was slow in society, so it could remain slow in the craftsman-like organizational structures. There was a sense of timelessness in business. It would be very difficult to find an environment in today's world that would be hospitable to an equilibrium organization.

Continuing to paddle down the river in an orderly fashion becomes a problem only if the current picks up. If the river becomes turbulent but the rowers keep paddling normally, a tension builds between the rowers and the river's flow. It becomes more and more difficult to stay on course. The result can be catastrophic. Either the boat snaps to meet the river's demands or it crashes on the rocks.

Alfred Hubler, the Assistant Director for the Center for Complex Systems Research at the University of Illinois has studied this phenomenon in his research on the control of chaos. One of Hubler's experiments involved a simulation of the stock market. The market is recognized as a chaotic system, so it functions like a white water river. Hubler assumed that decisions leading to movements in the stock market were made by a small group of leaders, who were closely watched by the rest of the herd. Hubler learned from his simulation that when the leaders used balancing feedback to control the movement of the stock market, a difference would build between the market and the leaders' target. The difference would build up like a sand pile. As with landslides that emerge on the sand pile, the simulated market experienced periodic crashes that would bring the investments in line with market behavior. The extent and frequency of the crashes were unpredictable.[63]

Equilibrium organizations run into trouble when a disparity develops relating to the amount of change happening in any of the organization's domains and other parts of the system. The more this happens, the more "problems" develop. *A problem exists when there is a difference between the behavior of the organization and the current needs of the system.*

If there is frequent change in one domain (such as the market place) and it is not matched in the others, the organization is headed for a catastrophe. The organization is not learning, it will not be able to adapt.

---

63 During the 1980s, Rene Thom developed a methodology for investigating major, discontinuous changes such as this. His work led to the field of catastrophe theory. Unfortunately, consideration of the theory was brief—until chaos theory came along. The work by Hubler and others on the control of chaos has a clear link to Thom's earlier work. Much credit is due Thom's protégé, Stephen Guastello, for his work integrating catastrophe theory into complex systems studies.

This is one of the great lessons of the Russian Revolution of 1988.[64] The basic tenet of the Soviet Union's management of its economy was central control. Manufacturing and agricultural targets were developed from the Kremlin in Moscow without consideration of differences in local conditions, the weather's unpredictability, or other factors which would lead to universal failure to meet the goals. The situation was so bad that it became a joke. Moscow would create a five-year plan, the collectives would accomplish whatever was possible, but they would then report having achieved the plan. Does this sound any different than experiences in many of our own companies?

At the same time, the Soviet Union's environment, its surrounding countries, was rapidly changing. Europe, the US, and Japan had moved into the age of rapid communications and advanced manufacturing techniques. Although the Soviet Union attempted to keep its borders information tight, the information age and the need to compete economically created extensive cracks in the Iron Curtain. Internet and fax communications with the West made it possible for the satellite countries, at least, to become aware of a materialistically better world. They demanded trade with the West when the Soviet Union could not keep pace. Reinforcing feedback loops developed involving commerce, science, and eventually political relations.

Mikhail Gorbechev's experiment in openness, Glasnost, was only the straw that broke the Soviet Union's back. Gorbechev hoped to use Glasnost to facilitate a change to a more modern, but still centralized economy. However, when a stocky carpenter jumped the wall at a shipyard in Gdansk to start Solidarity, the crack became visible within the satellite countries. Instead of controlled change, the Soviet Union experienced revolutionary change as the feedback cascaded into the unprepared center.

---

64 I first proposed the following analysis the Chaos Network Newsletter in November, 1991. Economist Robert Samuelson wrote a very similar analysis "The Way The World Works" in the January 12, 1998 edition of *NewsWeek* Magazine.

Entrepreneurial organizations and large established institutions have a tendency to function as equilibrium organizations. Entrepreneurial organizations, such as Digital Equipment Corporation under Ken Olsen's leadership, Apple Computers, or most recently Silicon Graphics, will base their direction on the vision of the founder or current CEO. Controls are established to reach the vision, regardless of surrounding events.

Silicon Graphics hit its high point during the second quarter of 1995 after achieving an excellent market advantage in the advanced graphical computing market. Their success came from deals with Nintendo and Time Warner and having been featured for visual effects in a number of films. In May of that year, Ed McCracken established a mission to increase sales by 36% to 50% annually. New equipment was planned, the company acquired other companies, and the company held off a takeover bid from Microsoft. (This sounds like the strategic plan for building automobiles described in Chapter 2.)

During the next several months, the company failed to take advantage of opportunities to evolve and adapt. Conditions changed, resulting in some of its partners failed to help it live up to its mission. Sun Computers became a formidable challenger and also bid to buy Silicon Graphics. Chip deliveries were delayed, and a top manager left to help run Netscape. Silicon Graphics ignored the potential of the Internet and lost money replacing defective chips. The company failed to change its mission, while all signals demonstrated a need to adapt.[65]

In October of 1997, Silicon Graphics announced a $56 million loss for the just completed quarter, resulting in a drop in stock value of over 10 points and the resignation of McCracken. The company became a takeover target, and faced a number of class action lawsuits alleging securities fraud. In January 1998, a new CEO was hired from Hewlitt Packard. While the company's technology remains state-of-the-art and

---

[65] Hof, Robert D. and Sager, Ira. "The Sad Saga of Silicon Graphics." *BusinessWeek*. August 4, 1997

is embarking on developing a series of collaborative alliances, the 1997 catastrophe will slow its ability to rebound making it questionable as to whether the alliances will result in a rebirth or acquisition by another company.

In similar fashion, Digital controlled the potential of change arising from new knowledge by such actions as restricting attendance at conferences to those running the sales booths. The excuse for this policy was financial. The decision actually supported maintaining the boat's direction toward CEO Ken Olsen's vision of centralized computing systems. The action restricted members from learning even a minimum about the directions being taken by competitors. As such, the company was not in a position to adapt to the decentralized decision making structures that was actually developing in corporations through personal computer usage. At one point in the early 1990's, this lack of networking and legal espionage caused the company to miss out participating in developing a unified platform for computer aided software engineering.

Digital's demise is a warning for Silicon Graphics. During the '90s, Digital was never able to fully rebound from losses that developed under Olsen's entrepreneurial leadership. The company did build a very strong service component, and continued to successfully maintain its core business at the mini-computer level. But in 1998, the company was bought out by Compaq, placing Compaq in direct competition with IBM, just as interest in server for the World Wide Web re-established interest in the mini and mainframe computer markets. It may yet turn out the Olsen's vision becomes correct, but on the totally different landscape of the World Wide Web.

Both cases represent the need for long term deviation from the founder's vision during regroupings within their industry. The fundamentals, a failure to build an infrastructure for adaptation, led the way to each company's demise.

Equilibrium organizations can be spotted easily. One often hears in meetings the saying, "if it ain't broke, why fix it" or, "we've got to stay the course." The performance management and compensation systems are designed to support consistency. If the organization has a quality program, it will be one of quality control based on inspections. Equilibrium organizations punish error and do not value diversity, knowing that both have the tendency to generate change.

Ironically, those working in equilibrium organizations often report a feeling of chaos, not calm. When I had the opportunity to make some presentations at Digital, for instance, I was presented with a "chaos" button, with a human face with hair sticking straight up!

Calling such experiences chaos is a misnomer. The feeling of chaos that workers at Digital, Silicon Graphics and General Motors experience actually develops from the tension that builds between the rowers' attempts to stay on course towards the mission and the natural direction that the river is taking. The tension is the energy spent to hold the system in check while it is preparing to explode.

I had the opportunity to manage a community health center that was operating at equilibrium. The organization had been started 25 years earlier as a free clinic for the local African-American community. It now provided primary health care to low income people throughout the county. One third of its funds came from the federal government, about half through fee payments including Medicare and Medicaid reimbursements, and the rest from local funding sources.

There were several pressures for the organization to change. The local health care system had changed from a three-hospital mix of public and private to a two-hospital competing system. The patient load had grown beyond the size of the facility and was no longer primarily African American, although the organization remained an African American institution. The health reimbursement system was converting to managed-care, and to stay competitive required some form of network development. The conversion to managed care, competition with the other two health systems, and the demands of local politics worked at odds to hold the organization at equilibrium.

From 1994 through 1997, the Center experienced at least four catastrophic events. Each catastrophe resulted from one side or another—the local political system, the federal government, and the local African American community—pushing to establish its vision for the direction of change. The last catastrophe was the loss of federal funding, an event which took place as attempts to change the relationships between the managed care environment and the health systems competition were underway. The final catastrophe resulted from the demands of the local political system to consolidate and gain centralized control of the social service delivery system in the county. These demands conflicted with the efforts to resolve the other system issues. The Center was not allowed to evolve naturally.

The interesting part of the case is what happened next. During the two months following the loss of the grant, the single point attractor began to spiral in tightly. The Center started to experience an implosion. It lost board members, staff, and clients. That was expected. What was unexpected was how the building started to also fall apart at the same time. The attractor seemed to affect inanimate objects along with the people involved.

Equilibrium organizations appear to be the ideal, but are no fun in reality.

Class 3 Rivers and Cyclical Organizations

The majority of today's organizations know that the river is no longer calm. Change is felt somewhere in the organization. Organizational designers have learned to build some flexibility into the ships of industry.

Class 3 rivers have long rapids that require intricate maneuvering. The course is hard to determine. Waves are high and irregular, there are strong cross currents, and eddies begin to develop. There are few rescue spots along the way and those in the boat require life jackets. However, once pulled off course, it is still possible to navigate back into the direction you had planned.

Navigation still helps on a Class 3 river. Either by scouting the course or by knowing the end point, it remains possible to plan a destination. Like temperature in a room controlled by a thermostat, boats on Class 3 rivers tend to go off course for short periods of time, but can return to the course with frequent adjustments.

Energy exists within the system on Class 3 rivers. The current is flowing, rowers do not have to row for the boat to move. However, the most effective rowing technique is not coordinated rowing, but individual rowing, especially through the rapids. At times, the current will pull the boat off course, even turn it around backwards. However, there are slow points where the raft can regain its direction.

The ideal predator-prey relationship between foxes and rabbits develops when the cycle of growth and diminishment of each population appears and is maintained. This is a sustainable and stable environment. At this point, the system is on a limit cycle attractor. In other words, while the system experiences change, it always returns to the same pattern of behavior over time.

Limit cycle or Class 3 behavior appears in organizations that realize there is a need to change. Management tries new things—starting quality circles this year and trying to be a learning organization the next. Attempts to change become so numerous that workers sometime complain about the latest "Management Flavor of the Month."

These organizations have established some connection with their environment, which motivates the attempts at change. Manufacturing companies often have links to technological and process changes. Service companies can be sensitive to their customers. Within these veins, some mutual evolution develops. Reinforcing feedback brings energy and information into the organization—it is aware of the changes. But balancing feedback dampens the impact of those changes. It keeps pulling the organization back on to its original track.

The assembly line and Frederick Taylor's notion of a scientific basis for management developed as an attempt to institutionalize and better form the equilibrium organization. But he developed his notions just as organizational systems were getting more turbulent. The pressures of industrialization, electricity and radio waves, wars and a developing economy made equilibrium systems inhospitable. The involvement of humans and their innate tendency towards nonlinear behavior also made the system unstable. Regardless of how hard the time/motion consultants tried, the system never operated exactly as planned.

Two factors worked together following World War 2 to move the environment beyond the calmness of a Class 1 river. First was recognition that humans could not be pigeonholed into linear job specifications. Experiments by social psychologists like those at General Electric's Hawthorne Plant established the need for a "human relations" approach to management. Second was the growing diversification of both the work place and the market.

Kurt Lewin interpreted the problems that organizations had achieving change as a natural resistance by humans to wanting to change. As described in Chapter 4, Lewin developed a model for change called the force field analysis. At the center of the model was the previously described linear equation, $F_R + F_E = 0$. Lewin's theory established that in order to bring about change, it was necessary to establish an imbalance between the two forces.

From the force field theory, Lewin and others determined that, to fight resistance, the change target needed to know what the results of the change would mean—what was at the end of the change process. This created the force that established mission and vision as the critical leadership role of the second half of this century. Picturing what was expected to be ahead in the river was expected to pull the individual or group along into the future.[66] Consultants offered training and assistance in reducing resistance to change as a central part of their services.

Jeffrey Goldstein, a professor in organization development at Adelphi University, studied Lewin's theory and found that it actually failed in practice. The way the force field is applied is that the group identifies one or more resistors and then makes a plan to reduce the power of that resistor. The problem is that reducing the force of resistance is also an act of change. Its implementation may also face secondary resistance, or it may not constitute enough of a change to effectively reduce the resistance. In either case, another analysis is required. This can become redundant as the idea of the little man inside one's brain having another little man inside his brain, ad infinitum.[67]

Goldstein eventually decided that resistance does not really exist. He called resistance "merely an initial and temporary attractor of the long-range developmental trajectory of a nonlinear system."[68] By this he meant that rather than resisting change, individuals and groups are attracted to some constellation of values, behaviors, and even habits that is functioning effectively for them at this point in time. In practice, a group continues to act in a certain way because it has the tools, knowledge, skills, and other resources to continue acting in that manner.

Application of the force field process actually pushes the organization into a limit cycle attractor. Each attempt to change is temporary. The attractor that Goldstein refers to usually pulls the organization

---

66 Lewin's change theory has dominated almost all western theories of change over the past fifty years. Most other popular theories, from Drucker's strategic planning and MBO process of the 1950's to the visioning entreaties of Stephen Covey and others, can be traced back to this theory. See, Michaels, Mark, "Chaos Theory and the Process of Change" in *What's New in Organization Development*

67 Goldstein, Jeffrey "A Far-From-Equilibrium Approach to Resistance to Change." *Organizational Dynamics 17(2): 16–22 (1988)*

68 Goldstein, Jeffrey, "The Unshackled Organization," p 58

back to where it started. Those times when change does develop using a force field analysis, as I will explain in detail shortly, are when an instability already exists in a system which would have resulted in change anyway. That happens most frequently when people already feel like they are in a sinking ship.[69]

The increase in diversity in both the work force and market is one of the factors pushing organizational systems towards change. In this instance, diversity not only refers to differences in race, sex, and religion, it includes differences in culture, values, skills, communication styles, educational experience, all the way to the level of individual perspective.

Diversity is one pressure that, by definition, breaks the symmetry of equilibrium. Diversity can even be a measure of the extent to which chaos exists within a system. The greater the diversity, the greater the chaos.

The role played by diversity in fostering chaos is a major reason why it is so strongly resisted by managers. In equilibrium and cyclical organizations, the demand to deal with differences takes the manager's time away from keeping the system on its pre-determined course. This was probably the real reason behind the actions taken by the Society for Human Resource Management (previously the American Society for Personnel Administration) to resist the establishment of laws and regulations instituting affirmative action in the 1960's and early 1970's. Its members were not racist. But they recognized the cost that would be involved to select and train a diverse group of individuals to work together towards shared goals—to fit round, star, and other shaped pegs into the already existing square holes. Adaptation would actually change the work place, and the

---

69 As previously noted, Tom Peters and others suggest that a constant state of crises needs to exist or be fabricated in organizations in order to insure that change will happen. In his latest book, *The Cycle of Innovation*, Peters took this one step further, proclaiming that "Destruction is cool." It will shortly become apparent that this is both not true (being a frequently incorrect interpretation of chaos theory) and is very dangerous to the long-term viability of the organization.

best that the human resource managers could hope for was to find ways to pull the altered boat back in line with the vision.[70]

Eventually, diversity made the river more turbulent than just Class 3. The boat began pushing outside of its planned course. People started crying out, "how can we still go towards our vision while being flexible enough to accommodate the diversity?"

The control-based answer has been to use values and culture management as a means towards allowing deviation while keeping the boat somewhat in the planned direction. The amount of deviation allowed differs from organization to organization. Values management has resulted in establishing bounded instability within organizations with the goal of maintaining a focused, Class 3 organization.

The Walt Disney Company under its founder scrutinized job applicants to insure that only those who could emulate its values would be hired. The new recruits were then subjected to a heavy dose of indoctrination into the company's culture. Disney's values were pushed upon the new employee. With the employment theme that all employees are "on stage", this established a similar dynamic as the relationship between the director and an actor. The director sets the boundaries of style for the performance, while the actor uses her skills to craft the individual part—bounded instability.

In some organizations, the values indoctrination process is so intense that practitioners from religions which may not agree with the values, complain that the company is violating their religious freedom. The fear of such charges at NASA's Lewis Research Center, caused the Center's

---

70 In the end, diversification of the workforce was the best thing that ever happened to the profession. Personnel Management in the 1950 and sixties focused on hiring, policy development, and firing. In smaller organizations, it was usually done by a clerical assistant. Workforce diversity caused the profession to become accountable, bringing in the need for measurement of effectiveness. This, along with the increased knowledge necessary for compliance with a growing body of legal regulation, increased the knowledge and role of the function. Personnel administration grew into human resource management, and its practitioners now participate on the executive team with equal status as financial management.

training staff to be wary of all but the most traditional management development projects. It was also reported that the Federal Aviation Administration might have gone over the line with a program that it provided employees.[71]

Class 3 organizations use pre-defined values to establish the boundaries of behavior and decision. Deviation is allowed within these boundaries, thereby allowing for a sense of diversity. But the boundaries restrict the potential of true diversity as they attempt to keep the organization on course. As with an equilibrium organization, if someone sees the river turning, but the planned course is straight, he best be quiet if he doesn't want to get thrown in the river. Of course by keeping quiet, the others would soon join him in the river anyway.

It is hard to see beyond the cyclical mental model of the world. The image of our world is all around us. Disney's movie, *The Lion King* celebrates the circle of life, Our method for keeping time is circular—the clock, the calendar, the seasons. There is birth, taxes, and death. The image feels instinctive. While our mental image is built from our sense of the sun going around the earth, it is squarely supported in the Newtonian sense—a view of time in which time can go both forward and backward.

We are entering into the age of exploring a new mental model. We are just starting to explore our universe in terms beyond circles, where there is a single direction of time along side and greater in importance than the bi-directional arrow, where creation is ongoing. It will significantly alter how we look at and lead organizations as well.

---

71 Usually these claims are made by Fundamentalist Christians against so-called New Age teachings. However, the issue can cut both ways. Stephen Covey's prescriptions are based on the tenets of the Mormons, and appear to have no research base to their claims for effectiveness, although they feel good. As the millennium drew near, there was a general drift towards practicing religion of some sort within organizational environments.

Class 6 Rivers and Adaptive Organizations on the Edge of Chaos

Class 6 rivers are distinguished by their long, continuous rapids. The rapids continue on, giving little time to breathe, let alone time to think. The waves are very high, irregular and unavoidable, making it almost impossible to see very far ahead. The situation is life threatening. We have reached the edge of chaos.

The movement from the craft age to the industrial age represented the movement of business systems to a Class 3 environment. The movement into the information age, and from nationalism to a global economy has taken us into Class 6 waters.

During the agricultural and crafts age, everything in the world was spread out. People, countries, and systems did not bump into each other often. The shrinking of time for communicating over great distances has now made it impossible for people, countries and cultures not to bump into each other. Like molecules of air in a shrinking balloon, the originally stable relationships have become short term and unpredictable. It is just like riding through waves where you cannot see ahead. All you can do is paddle to stay alive.

We have reached the status that most of us fear. We are at the point of no control, the point of unpredictability. The initial temptation is to find a way to pull back. Like Dupont's experience with its film-thinning machine in Chapter 2, we want to slow the system down. But we can't, its speed is out of our hands.

Organizations have yet to figure out how to survive in such turbulence. Peters' prescription for thriving on chaos, which emphasized customer responsiveness, increasing the pace of innovation, and empowering people, was only part of the solution. Senge added another piece to the puzzle by introducing system dynamics with positive and negative feedback, showing how the connections between these systems interact.

The first practical solution became applying these concepts to the reinvention of the organization. This was first proposed by Peters' first co-author, Robert Waterman.[72] But reinvention is not much different than the death experienced by the ninety percent of entrepreneurial organizations that failed to become reinvented. It usually requires new people, equipment, and markets to succeed. How does that differ from the death of one and birth of another organization?

The concept that organizations can be reinvented has its roots in the organizational life cycle. The organizational life cycle is an extension of what is known as the product life cycle. The product life cycle is defined by four measurable stages of sales history that a product experiences including start-up, growth, maturity, and decline. For a one-product company, the organizational life cycle is dependent upon the product life cycle. To overcome the cycle and save a company, a second product is started before the first product reaches decline.

The organizational life cycle is nonlinear. However, when one follows the logic of reinvention, the overall outcome is cyclical—the process of start-up to decline just keeps repeating itself. Reinventing organizations can be effective for organizations in Class 3 environments. But reinvention is just as traumatic as merger and acquisition.

The need for speed makes reinvention impossible when the rapids reach the Class 6 stage, when there is no time to think. Just as Dupont was forced to find a new way to design the knife so that they could speed up their film making process, we must look for new ways to run organizations in order for them to survive the white water rapids.

The problem is not hopeless. Three dynamics of Class 6 environments, also known as weakly chaotic systems, provide hope and a new strategy for survival. To understand these, let's first return to the relationship between rabbits and foxes.

---

72 Waterman, Robert. *The Renewal Factor*

The predator-prey model is actually a well-controlled experiment. Other variables that exist in the real world are left out of the equation. Where are other predators, like bears? What about disease and the weather? As described in Chapter 2, it was previously impossible to experiment and understand systems with anything but a highly limited number of variables. In this case, when a second predator is added, for instance, the system becomes very unstable. Under traditional projections, the system is out of control. It becomes impossible to predict the ratio of rabbits to foxes for any given point in time.

The first Class 6 dynamic is that it is possible to evaluate the system when it is in chaos. As described earlier, just when the system loses a sense of order on traditional graphs, a chaotic attractor appears in phase space. It is the chaotic attractor that controls the boundaries and possibilities of the system. The wildness disappears. With this information, the organization can at least understand the scope and potentials of the landscape.

The second dynamic is the explosion of diversity at the edge of chaos, the emergence of the random repertoire of possibilities. Chaos mathematician Mitchell Feigenbaum explains that at the edge of chaos, all potential outcomes for a system become possible. We are generally used to there only being one right answer. But at the edge of chaos, many answers are possible. The key is allowing one that works to emerge.

Hubler's experiments with the stock market suggest a method for finding solutions to problems for systems at the edge of chaos. Hubler found that the way to survive in a weakly chaotic environment was to instill weak chaos in the system that corresponds to such an environment.

Weak chaos is a natural phenomenon. It is what results from experimentation, from making mistakes which become successes, and from the diversity of ideas, values, and abilities which exist in any naturally formed group of individuals.

For instance, when rafting, the key lesson going through rapids is to paddle or die. Anyone who has rafted knows that it is not important that everyone paddle in the same direction. In fact, that is a recipe for disaster. If, instead, each person paddles based on the conditions at his/her station, the boat gets through. Sometimes it is turned around, but it does get through.

Peters suggests that it is important to maintain a sense of urgency to keep an organization from becoming complacent. To accomplish this, many companies will frequently reorganize or create some other artificial emergency. CEO's knowing that I speak about chaos, have frequently brought me into their organizations believing that I would provide an impetus for creating this sense of urgency. But such unrealistic chaos is counter-productive.

Hubler describes strong and unexpected chaos as being like taking a china pendulum and hitting it with an iron mallet. Followers in the stock market simulation who are exposed to such behavior become distrustful of the leaders and search for new leaders. Similarly, in such organizations we frequently find high turnover rates from burned out staff.

Hubler's mathematical explanation of weak chaos is best understood by thinking of hits and misses. In the next three figures, consider the points to be possible products that the market place desires. The points on the line represent different products developed by a company to respond to market needs. In Figure 5-1, the company is single-minded, producing only one product. As you can see, his/her chances of success are very small. That is the controlled or visionary approach.

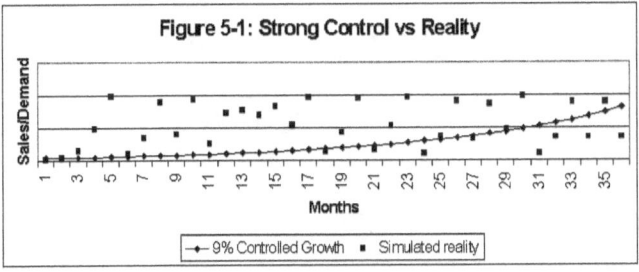

Figure 5-1: Strong Control vs Reality

Figure 5-2, the approach is completely random. There are hits in this instance. But the effort to achieve these hits is extensive, The actual number of hits turns out to be less than in weakly chaotic systems. The company spends too much money trying to find a market while not receiving enough in return.

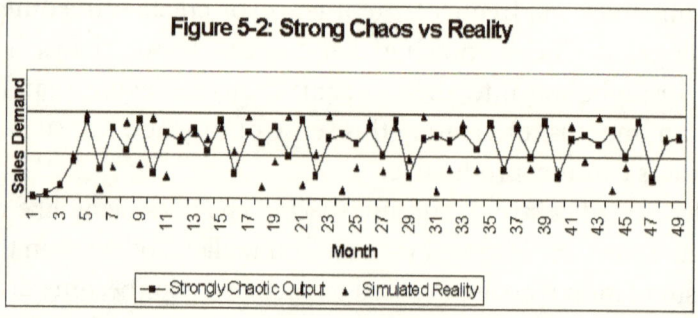

Figure 5-3 shows a weaker approach to the chaotic environment. The results are more hits with less effort. If the company is trying to find one product that will sell, it is more likely to achieve that quest by testing out a number of products, first. If it is trying to stay afloat over time, than enough of its products will succeed to allow this to happen.

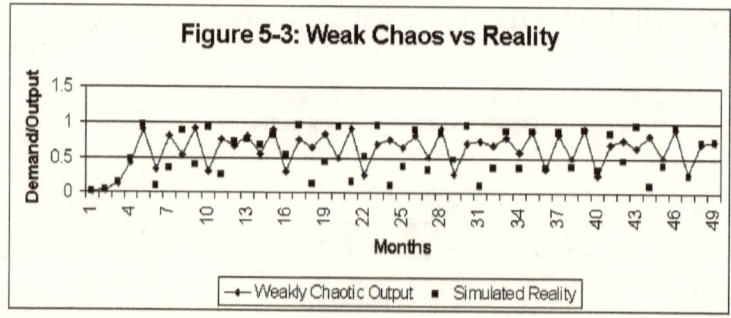

Similarly, when each person paddles, based on his/her immediate need, the group as a whole is more responsive to the changing currents. If the situation were static, one could think of the process of using chaos to dampen the impact of the chaos. It is probably more appropriate to think of the situation as establishing a sense of resonance between the rafters and their environment.[73]

What is really happening here is self-organization. The chaotic attractor defines the boundaries of self-organization. The effectiveness of the results are defined by the development of an evolutionary reinforcing loop between the system and its environment.

Many companies are innovative, yet they also die. Apple Computers and Digital are both innovative. Yet at this writing, Apple is balanced on the brink of extinction and Compaq has acquired Digital. Digital had been one of Peters' Excellent companies in 1980.[74]

Much has been written about the 3M Corporation. 3M is over 90 years old. It shows up as a model of excellence in all of Tom Peters' works. The company has generated growth over most of its long history. During most of that time, the company did not have a vision. Its current vision is simple, to foster innovation. The statement does not meet any of our definitions of vision statements. All it really says is that the company has always succeeded by adaptation, so it will keep on adapting.

The key difference between 3M and Digital is not the fact of innovation but the breadth of it. At Digital, innovation was confined to the narrow scope of Ken Olsen's technological vision. Everybody had to

---

73 For people management, two examples of this strategy come to mind, basket ball teams and jazz groups. For application of the first, see Robert Kreidel's *Game Plans*. For the latter see Redding, John and Catalenello, Ralf. *Strategic Readiness: The Making of a Learning Organization.*

74 Two years after publication of In Search of Excellence, BusinessWeek ran a cover article recognizing that over fifty percent of the companies defined as excellent in Peters' book no longer fit the criteria. Peters even recognized the problem in his opening to Thriving on Chaos (p3). Now, while companies like Sears and K-Mart are on the brink, many others no longer exist, including DEC, Wang Labs, Lockheed, Gould, and Atari.

paddle in the direction of centralized computing, even when the direction changed to personal computing.

Long-lived organizations demonstrate a natural ability to develop evolutionary links that enable ongoing adaptation. Many of the DOS innovations, from hard drives to mice, modems, and the Internet, happened outside of IBM/Microsoft. Then the innovations were quickly incorporated into later versions of the product. The environment for innovation spread beyond just the corporation boundaries, establishing an extensive diversity of possibilities.

Apple Computers, on the other hand, centralized innovation around a specific product vision—the Apple IIe and then the Macintosh. At the same time, the cloning of DOS based machines outside of IBM allowed for more extensive innovation than would have been possible just within IBM. Even Apple's founder, Steve Jobs had to leave the company to create a new, innovative computer, the NeXt computer.

Like many long-lived consumer product companies like Proctor and Gamble, 3M thrives on its diversity of innovation. 3M started out making sandpaper, which is a product requiring minerals, an adhesive and paper. Each of the three resources blossomed into other products. The most talked about recent innovation was, of course, the PostIt Note, which was the result of research on adhesives. Now, 3M is creating innovative products from PostIt Notes while continuing to create other new products in distinctly different markets.

Such diversity is the hallmark of survival on Class 6 rivers. Diversity allows for a faster reaction to changes in the environment. The reaction may even appear unconscious and automatic. This results in the ability to adapt more quickly to the environment.

However, the diversity is not all out chaos. The capabilities and history of each company bound the chaos. Penn Central's diversification purchasing financial institutions in 1968 was seen by some as the cause of its downfall. However, the purchase fit into the capability of the company because of its large real estate holdings as a railroad. Had it chosen to purchase hospitals, for which it had few comparable tags, the company probably would not have survived. Staying within the boundaries distinguishes between the use of weak chaos for adaptation and the destructively strong chaos currently proposed by Peters.

In each of these examples, it becomes apparent that successful products do not create new markets, as visionaries would like to suggest. Instead, they become successful because they are sucked into a market niche, a constellation of potential and possibly unrecognized demand that develops from potential created within the existing market. If the world is not ready for the product, the product will hang on the vine either till there is interest or the product dies.[75]

In the Post-It Notes story, a failed experiment creating a new adhesive did, in fact, hang on the vine under its originally planned use. The glue used on the notes was originally developed for another product that was dropped. Then another experiment led its developer to create paper that temporarily adheres to other paper, and keeps its stickiness when removed. Still, at first only a small group of secretaries used the notes. Of course, once the potential for the product was realized, 3M created one heck of a marketing strategy! Now, even executives have found uses from jotting down changes in draft letters to book marks, to plastering reminders all around their computers. (When I need to remember an assignment from my wife, I'll write it on a PostIt Note and stick it to my shirt until I leave the office.) Many of us would rather give up our telephones than our PostIt Notes.

To some, PostIt Notes represented a renewal of 3M's marketing touch. The contrary is truer. 3M was already well positioned in numerous other markets ranging from video tape to medical equipment. PostIt Notes was only one experiment that worked—many others failed.

---

75 This explains why the saying, "If you build a better mousetrap..." has never worked in reality.

Conclusion

When an organization finds that its behavior is out of sync with its environment, it needs to find a way to change that behavior. The traditional approach has been to fight resistance by decreasing the forces resisting change. The process usually involved identifying where the organization wants to be as opposed to where it stands now—a gap is usually identified to encourage change. For equilibrium and cyclical organizations, the strategy appears to be correct, since the end result is the desired change.

The story of the white water presents a slower, yet more trustworthy alternative. Instead of attempting to plan a predictable outcome, the solution is to build more diversity into the organization. There are a number of possible strategies for achieving this. First, research and development projects, including skunk works are a critical source of change. They should be ongoing, particularly if management can quickly recognize when to pull the plug on a project.

Information needs to come into the organization regularly. It can come in from the outside through attendance at conferences, access to the Internet, point of sale data collection systems, and even placing more outside directors on a board. Adding new people from different industries also helps (hopefully without dismissing existing staff). Diversity in terms of culture, race, sex, and background must be considered a business asset, as well.

Also, begin experiments in different parts of the organization. This represents the underlying success of quality circles, which then prepared a number of companies to be ready for Total Quality Management (while others, which never tried the first, were woefully unprepared for the latter). Rather than instituting "the right" new policy, observe policy implementation in various parts of the organization to see which are really being implemented.

Regardless of the strategy, it is critical to provide an information infrastructure so that the results of experiments can be shared. This provides the reinforcing feedback loops that bring the organization to the edge of chaos ready for reorganization.

Automation of the workplace provides a perfect case comparison of the effectiveness of the traditional and complex systems approaches to change, demonstrating the supremacy of the latter. During the 1980s, most organizations moved from manual clerical assistance to personal computers and networking. The standard approach was to announce to the staff that computers would be brought in, staff would receive training, and then the staff was expected to adapt to the new work style. The approach failed universally. Companies experienced sabotage, health and stress reactions, and down right refusal to use the equipment. There are many stories about computers sitting unused on desks for months while the workers would return to using their trusty typewriters.

The companies that succeeded demonstrated a longer history of change. Usually, a few "techie" types either requested and received or brought in their own computers. Friends would stop over and see the quality of their work and ask how to accomplish similar results. The friends would then insist on computers for their desks. Use spread like a slow burning wild fire until companies were faced with networking many different brands of computers. Only by that time, the workers were ready to join in the change, and conversion to networked systems went smoothly.

Chapter 6

The Emergence of Fitness

On a class six river, everyone paddles for their lives. That they may paddle in different directions actually helps them survive. How does it get them down the river safely?

The answer takes us back to the pot of spaghetti in Chapter 2. The chaotic bubbles are the turbulent environment. The spaghetti's response emerges through self-organization.

Self-organization is the process of creation in the new creation story. Self-organization happens at all levels of reality. It explains how quanta interact to form atoms, how atoms interact to form molecules, and how four undifferentiated cells can continue to divide until a human being is formed. It is the underlying dynamic enabling survival in ecological niches. And it is the reason why social systems develop, prosper, and die.

One of the first scientists to discuss self-organization was Ilya Prigogine. Prigogine received the Nobel Prize for identifying self-organization in turbulent flows, such as oil pipelines. He called such systems "dissipative structures," because they dissipated entropy into the environment, warding off decay and the tendency towards equilibrium.

The notion of self-organization developed concurrently in several disciplines. Chemists and physicists identified auto-catalytic sets which now serve as the basis for self-repairing metals and new, stronger bonding materials. In biology, Kauffman, Dawkins and others theorized how the first organic molecules developed through self-organization, eventually leading to the emergence of DNA. Umberto Maturana studied rain forests and other ecological systems, identifying the self-organized relationships between subsystems, calling such relationships autopoietic systems. In mathematics and computer science, John Holland and others experimented with self-organization, inventing the cellular automata described in Chapter 2 and turning them into artificial life programs and other simulations such as SimCity and SimEarth. Umberto Huberman and associates at Xerox PARC used similar computer models to simulate social behavior in human beings.

There is nothing magical about self-organization. It is a function of fitness, probability, and reinforcing feedback.

Self-organization as a Function of Fitness

Turn off the heat below the spaghetti and the strands fall randomly to the bottom of the pot. Without an ongoing source of energy, self-organization cannot be sustained. Without energy, the system falls back to equilibrium. So job one for any complex adaptive system, such as an organization, is to make certain that it has a continual source of energy.

At the grossest level, organizational energy comes in as cash income, since that is what is required to obtain most other resources. During this century, information has emerged as an energy source on par with the need for cash. The two are just as important to organizational survival as food is to an explorer's survival.

However, this description is too simplistic. A more accurate understanding or energy flow within an organizational system considers the various potential sources of energy. For instance:

- Financial energy—capital to finance the acquisition of other resources

- Energy from the marketplace—customers willing to purchase the products or services
- Internal, human energy—individuals who perform the work required to make the product or service (In science, work is defined as the energy needed to move an object.)
- Physical energy—the physical resources needed to produce the product or service
- Technologically driven energy—processes which can efficiently be employed to build the product

Organizations can also receive energy in the form of information. Information can be defined in terms of knowledge of the energy source. It can also be explained as feedback from other parts of the system. If information flows between sub-systems, then the feedback is reinforcing. If the information is curtailed, then the feedback is balancing. Reinforcing feedback becomes critical to vitalize new activity within any part of the organization.

Fitness was defined as being the state in which *an organization's process is in line with those required of the system at a given point in time to enable its survival.* Since survival requires energy, survival depends on making certain reinforcing feedback loops exist within the system. To survive, the system—organization—must respond to the system's needs so that there is a flow of energy into and through the system. Such information, in addition to money, is a critical mode of exchange in any form of commerce.

Fitness exists when a system reaches a functional relationship with its environment, enabling an adequate level of energy flow for survival. There are various potential levels of fitness within an environment. The distribution of that potential is the fitness landscape shown in Figure 3-1.

The traditional notion of survival of the fittest implies that there is a point when all the parts within a system—within an ecological niche in biology—reach the ideal symbiotic relationship. Those not fitting into that relationship do not survive.

At the core of the third creation story is the understanding that everything continues to change. Individual degrees of fitness and the fitness landscape participate in the changing Universe. Accordingly, fitness must also change over time.

In the predator-prey system, problems develop when another predator comes on the scene. This changes the fitness landscape by requiring that the existing energy be distributed among more participants. All participants become endangered until a new set of relationship develops.

The same is true for organizational relationships. The amount of energy available at any point in time is finite. Acquisition of energy one place means a loss elsewhere. Search for new energy sources must begin. The ever-changing fitness landscape is what makes organizational survival a continual matter of exploration.

Symphony orchestras are currently figuring out how to adjust to a changing landscape. Orchestras started to develop around 1600 AD and grew up with the industrial age. This is not just a coincidence since the great orchestras and orchestral pieces are representative of the Newtonian, mechanical schemata. The score is the strategic plan of the composer. The product, a musical presentation, is achieved through carefully following of the plan. Just as others easily replace factory workers on the assembly line, so long as the replacement has the same skills, another who is skilled at playing the same instrument can easily replace one musician. The orchestra musician is a tool in the composers system just as the mechanic became another tool in the factory of scientific management.

To appreciate a great symphony requires the time and effort to sit and listen. Such time was still available in the 19th and early 20th century, especially for the rich. Energy flowed, and was even incorporated into the great pieces by Beethoven or Stravinsky. Now, who has time to sit, listen, and concentrate? As we run from place to place, there is too much noise and too little time, not even 30 minutes to listen to a regular symphony. Our interests are short paced, MTV 3 minute videos with 10 second images are more our speed.

The energy is draining out of the great orchestras. Orchestras like the Philadelphia, which was grandest under Leopold Stokowski, now play to empty seats. Most orchestras are located in major metropolitan areas, yet those patrons with money flee to the suburbs as soon as the sun goes down. Government support, which was promised to maintain our national musical treasures, has disappeared as interest in arts conflicts with interest in the commercial culture. Union musicians and orchestra management squabble over the dwindling resources, forgetting their original love for music. And the almost religious belief in the product has kept boards, management, and staff from acquiring the reinforcing feedback necessary to allow emergent change. Instead, catastrophic change breaks out with strikes and bankruptcies, followed by incremental changes.

Some individuals and orchestras are beginning to respond creatively to the problem. Around 1990, George Maull, an entrepreneurial conductor, founded the Philharmonic Orchestra of New Jersey. Located in Northern New Jersey, the orchestra's potential seemed limited by competition from across the Hudson River in New York City. But New York orchestras were experiencing the same losses as all other orchestras.

Maull's orchestra was blessed with two special problems. It did not have a large auditorium that could become its permanent residence. Moreover, it could not afford a permanent, full paid cadre of musicians. As a result, Maull was forced to improvise. He called his strategy chaotic.

What Maull did was to diversify his concert structure. This included diversifying the repertoire to include pieces requiring different size orchestras, diversifying the location of concerts, and even the form of concerts—from romantic valentine dinner concerts to traditional set ups.

Maull started with no funds, his dedicated wife Marcia, and his idea. While today the orchestra still does not rival the New York Philharmonic, that is not his goal. The orchestra is now financially solvent and attracts corporate sponsorship. More importantly, being listener sensitive, the orchestra is reaching individuals who, otherwise, would not be interested in classical music. The best measure of success is the growth of Maull's courses on music appreciation, which has developed as an outgrowth of his recognition of audience interest coupled with lack of knowledge. Regardless, the orchestra is always in a position to move along the fitness landscape.

The Likely Solution is the Probable Solution

Statistics plays a significant role in self-organization. Chapter 1 discussed how, when rolling a pair of dice, there is a greater probability that a six will be rolled over a two or a twelve. In the same light, a person playing the card game War who holds the greater number of aces at the beginning will, more often than not, be the winner. The random acts of war in the game are the element, which tries to equalize this opening inequality.

Richard Morley, the inventor and entrepreneur who is the father of the programmable controller, applies another statistical approach to succeed as a venture capitalist. Morley has only three basic rules for evaluating each company in which he invests:

1) There must be three "gurus" working on the project (although only one should have a Ph.D.);
2) The product/service should have control of 100% of its market (by owning the patent, for instance); and,
3) There should be a potential return of ten times the investment.

Morley maintains his portfolio so that he loses money on 80 percent of the companies in which he invests. He calls this his "failure rate," which, to him, is the most important investing statistic. By managing the failure rate instead of individual investments, Morley is assured of a profit of at least 11 percent over time.

Morley likens the strategy to betting on horse races. He explains that if you are betting on a race with 10 horses and each bet returns $10 for a $1 bet, then if you bet on all the horses in the race (total bet $10), you are guaranteed to break even, always winning back your $10. By managing a failure rate of 80, Morley cheats the banker by insuring that 2 horses always win. The result is to win $20 on $10 in bets over time.

Morley admits that at any given time, the failure rate may actually be more or less than 80 percent. That is where the "law of large numbers" comes into play.

The law of large numbers states that the greater the number of events, the closer the average results will come to the predicted (statistical) mean. Tossing a coin demonstrates the law.

Each time you flip a coin, you have a 50-50 chance that the coin will come up heads. Just because it came up heads does not mean that it will definitely come up tails the next flip, however. In fact, if you toss the coin only 10 times, it is more likely that the distribution of all tosses will be something other than 5 heads and 5 tails. It would not be unusual if you pulled four heads in a row.

However, if you toss the coin 100 times, you can safely bet that overall, the spread will be somewhere between 35 and 65 heads (a 30% range). If you toss the coin 1 million times the spread will narrow to between 497,000 to 503,000, heads, which is only a 0.6% range. If any other results develop, you have a reason to question the honesty of the coin.

Accordingly, the investor cannot assess his/her winnings based on just a few investments, when following Morley's formula. The results are assessed over the long term instead. After 100 investments, the investor who uses this strategy will have a high chance of earning an average of $20 (plus or minus 15% of $20) for every $10 invested.

Morley admonishes companies that work by managing their successes instead of their failures. Most companies fail to recognize the value of these rules and limit the number of research investments that they make to those which they feel have the greatest chance of success. Morley recommends that the companies invest less per project over a larger number of projects in order to succeed, rather than trying to guess which one will succeed. Based on the numbers, following this approach guarantees long term success.

The lesson here represents an important shift in management thinking. Organizations traditionally think in terms of looking for the best way, the right way, the one way to succeed. His/her vision is the one to be followed, and others trust that it will bring success. Funders back entrepreneurs who have one success, believing that the once successful entrepreneur got there because s/he had the right stuff. Morley's prescription is to forget individual cases and set up a portfolio of projects without regard to the past performance of any one individual. When properly built, the portfolio as a whole is guaranteed to be a winner.

Applied to organizational strategy, setting up a portfolio means building a diversity of possibility—a random repertoire of possibility—into the organization. For years, creativity experts have cajoled companies to take such steps as rewarding failure and being prepared to try many different strategies, if they expected to identify the right strategy. However, these pleadings were made only for situations that required a creative response. Now, organizations must realize that the dynamics of creativity—diversity—is the very basis of survival.

Total quality management works effectively in conjunction with self-organization when it is interpreted as a continuing search on the fitness landscape. This is how Deming's approach functions with the "plan-do-check-act" cycle. Rather than just continual quality, it becomes continual adaptation. But the concepts of zero defects or six sigma, benchmarking, and "sticking to the knitting" remove all the diversity from within the system. The extent of diversity is another way to measure the extent of chaos in a system. Limiting diversity is another way to limit the adaptability of the system.

Change Emerges

Kauffman explains that life emerged over time as the result of random interactions between molecules. The interactions became frequent enough, and the chemicals that interacted became abundant enough to cause carbon-based or organic molecules. These continued bouncing against each other frequently enough that amino acids and, eventually DNA formed. [76] From a random repertoire of possibilities eventually came life.

The law of large numbers was critical in this process. Had chemicals other than carbon and oxygen been more abundant, then something else would have happened. Helping the process along was reinforcing feedback. As more carbon molecules emerged, this led to a greater ability to produce more carbon molecules.

The same process works in organizations. Consider the simple process of making a decision. Suppose a manager has to make an important decision. If there are 150 employees in his organization, at least 150 possible solutions are available to him. This diversity-the random repertoire of possibilities—faces any system poised at the edge of chaos.

A random selection is made from the possible choices. Because the manager has met only 50 others in the company due to his random interactions, s/he knows something about how these 50 people think. So s/he decides to draw his/her task force from within that fifty. The manager has just eliminated 100 other possible solutions. From the fifty, 15 beg off meeting because of other commitments and s/he eliminates 15

---

76 Kauffman ibid. ppgs 14 - 59

for various reasons like personality conflicts or status. Twenty people agree to participate in making this decision. When the meeting is held, another five do not show. We are now down to only 15 possible answers at the first meeting—10 percent of the number we started with!

Reinforcing feedback: the selected potential solutions iterate to conclusion—with the unpredictable results being defined by small differences in starting conditions.

Scene 1—The Seed: Through discussion at the meeting the manager realizes that 3 people were thinking along one line (A), 5 along a second line (B), 2 along a third line (C), 4 on a fourth idea (D), and the manager had one idea (E). The group decides to break up into research teams and meet again in a week.

Scene 2—The First Iteration: At the next meeting, five from the first meeting failed to show, while the five who missed the first meeting made it. Of the five no-shows, 2 were from group A, and three were from group D. Of the new members, 2 support B, 2 support C, and 1 supports A. The manager also changed his/her position to A. (A=3, B=7, C=4, D=1, E=0). The group decides to no longer consider E or D, and further research is done on A, B, and C.

Scene 3—The Second Iteration: At the next meeting, there are again 5 no-shows and 5 returnees. The no-shows include the 1 D supporter, 2 supporters of B, and 2 supporters of C. The returnees include the 2 from group A and the 3 from the first group D, who insist on reconsideration of D. The new lay out is, A=5, B=5, C=2, D=3. Recognizing that the major split is between A and B, C and D are dropped. There is further research.

Final Scene—The Third Iteration: At the final meeting, everyone shows up. Those not changing in A and B line up as follows: A=5, B=7. Consequently, A's presentation is reflective of 50 person hours work, while B's used 70 person hours work. Of the 8 undecideds, the extra time on B's presentation swayed 5 while 3 were swayed to A. B became the accepted decision.

	Seed	Iteration 1	Iteration 2	Iteration 3
Group A	3	3	5	8
Group B	5	7	5	12
Group C	2	4	2	
Group D	4	1	3	
Group E	1	0	0	
AbsentA	1	2		
AbsentB	2		2	
AbsentC	2		2	
AbsentD		3	1	
AbsentE				
TotalA	4	5	5	8
TotalB	7	7	7	12
TotalC	4	4	4	
TotalD	4	4	4	
TotalE	1	0	1	

Reading through this apparently real life situation shows how, through reinforcing feedback—iterations in which results of a past meeting are inputted into the start of subsequent meetings—it appears as though A and B are the major competitors. The top third of the chart below further demonstrates such thinking, with the appearance that support for A continues to grow, yet is beat out by B at the wire. The bottom third of the chart shows a second dynamic—in which the real support stays constant and is greatest for B throughout the process. B started ahead, enabling it to stay ahead, again, like who has the most aces at the start of the card game War. In our case, the small difference in starting conditions between A and B iterated to B's favor.

Those disturbed by this example of decision making should consider potential ways to take advantage of this reality. Strategies include:

1. Pay less attention to who is assigned to participate in a decision and more to diversity of thinking within the group.

2. Surface conflict in the meetings to take advantage of differences instead of promoting consensus from the beginning.

3 Make sure less vocal participants get their ideas in, to offset the potential for herd behavior.

4 Trust the process—recognizing that this is an optimization process. The process resulted in the development of humans, for instance.

W. Brian Arthur is one of the developers of the theory behind this example of decision making. In his "Theory of Positive Returns," Arthur demonstrates how VHS beat BETA, a supposedly superior product, for control of the video camera industry. According to Arthur, a random, small difference in the planning meetings of the two competing companies—that JVC's meeting planning the VHS format included an individual knowledgeable of distribution, iterated into early development of a distribution system. This resulted in building an earlier demand for VHS, forcing more VHS systems to be produced.[77]

Natural organizational change works the same way, although not always as intended. While managers are trying to establish policies and controls, practices develop through experimentation and repeated usage. A machinist finds a better way to tool a piece of equipment. Or, as the earlier case on automating the work place showed, an individual tries using a computer and likes it. Eventually, others experiment and find the solution works. By the time the new method is made into a policy, it is already being used by most people.

These examples involve systems that are already operating on the edge of chaos. In most organizations, managers are taught to "manage change." In other words, they are taught that if the change does not fit into existing policies or goals, that it should somehow be eliminated. This use of balancing feedback controls change within the organization and restricts the natural evolution of the system.

---

77 Arthur, W. Brian, "Positive Feedback in the Economy", *Scientific American*, 2/90

Movement towards fitness tends to be a movement away from diversity. We previously considered how the personal computer market started as an explosion of different companies, equipment types, and operating systems. During the 20 years of market development, the market settled down to one key operating system—Windows. Windows was built on a DOS foundation from a MacIntosh like graphical interface. Once accepted in Windows 3.1, it became the primary software platform. This all happened as a result of the development of reinforcing feedback loops. DOS became the IBM operating system. IBM's distribution system gave it access to the lucrative business market, gaining market supremacy over Apple early. Licensing IBM/DOS technology to clone makers, who economically filled the demand that was outside of IBM's grasp, further enhanced the supremacy. Dominant market share made the introduction of Windows a manageable conversion, whereas interfacing with Apples became more cumbersome. Eventually, even Apple Computers was forced to find a way to live with the predominant company, Microsoft.

This process can be understood as an exploration of the fitness landscape until a fitness peak is reached. That peak may not be the highest, fittest peak. Many will continue to insist that the MAC/OS system is a higher peak. But it is good enough. All that is left are incremental improvements. There is no way to shake Microsoft off that peak

Another way to understand this process is to picture a group of bees, ants, or other insect swarming around a prey. Swarming is a search process that is dependent upon probability in the manner that was just described.

Picture a landscape with different level peaks. On the top of each peak, there is food. The higher the peak, the more food can be found at the top. The goal is to find and climb the peak with the most food as quickly as possible.

There are two ways to approach this problem. The traditional way is to have everyone charge up and conquer one peak together. When the food is expended, everyone then goes, together, to find another peak. This is the approach of visionary companies like Digital and Apple. Those who survive under this paradigm do so only by successfully practicing reinvention on a periodic basis. Clearly, when all the food on the peak is eaten, the whole group must go looking for another peak, the organization must be reinvented before it dies. In the mean time, another group may have already found, nested on, and taken control of a higher peak.

The process can be easily tracked within industries. The movie, *Those Magnificent Men in their Flying Machines* demonstrates how participants in the airplane industry swarmed until settling in on an effective airplane design. In the first quarter of the century, as the movie demonstrates, airplanes included bi-planes, tri-planes, front propeller driven, rear propeller driven, delta wings, and all sorts of other styles. Over time, one general style, the single-wing plane, began to dominate the industry. For another fifty years, that was seen as the highest peak on the landscape.

Once a high peak is reached, all who can fit on the peak join in. Design changes become incremental—the industry moves from revolution to innovation.

Organizations can also implement swarming. IBM used a truncated version when it developed its personal PC, establishing competitive skunk-works groups to experiment with different designs. Chapter 7 will describe how Ford inadvertently used the process in the early 1980s to spearhead its transformation.

Swarming must be a natural phenomenon, which takes advantages of reinforcing links with its environment. Otherwise, the results can be useless. A type of swarming explains the process used in popular large system change efforts such as Future Search and Open Space Technology. But in many of these cases, the process is directed in an isolated, intellectual environment—usually in a retreat setting of some sort—which only leads to everyone trying to run up the same peak together once the session is over.

These efforts start when consultants work to get "the whole system" in the room. The goal is to reach a group "vision" and a plan for implementing that vision.

Popular large system change programs replicate the manager's decision-making system described above. A group of facilitators work with a large group of stakeholders. They generate a large list of ideas, which include everyone's ideas. The list represents a landscape that is a projection of the participants' perceptions. It may or may not fit the actual landscape.

The facilitators than lead a search of the constructed landscape to find the statistically defined highest peak. Repetitive ideas on the list are given greater weight, allowing for their continued consideration. Through discussion, like-minded ideas are merged into compound/complex sentences. Peer pressure and the nature of the exercise lead to the eventual exclusion of potentially valuable information from those individuals "calling from the outlying peaks." Global concepts are developed which includes the thoughts of the majority, becoming accepted as the new vision. Since the landscape, itself is a construct, there is no demonstration that the vision has any relationship with what is happening in the real world.

Unfortunately, more often than not, the relationship between the vision and reality is so great, that the task groups lose their energy, wither away, and die. The incorrect diagnosis was that there was too much resistance to change.

Sometimes these sessions result in change despite the visioning sessions. True, the interpersonal dynamics of the session builds energy into a group that may have been marginal. But actual change develops in the implementation process. During implementation, which will occur over a long period of time, smaller task groups develop goals for implementing the vision. If the groups function well, then it is here that the process meets with reality. Implementation becomes a hodgepodge of projects, some of which work, some work after adjustments, and some fail. The real search on the fitness landscape has only started.

A more effective approach is to skip the large system change meetings. Instead, assign a group of independent task forces to address a problem. Make certain that there is communication between the groups. Let them proceed on their own and watch how change develops over time.

What happens when the landscape changes? The fact that experiments are again beginning on new airplane designs demonstrates that reaching a fitness peak does not mean that the swarm has settled on the most ideal peak forever. The landscape can and does change, making peaks transient.

Microsoft is facing this very question. The theory behind the antitrust litigation against Microsoft at the time of this writing is that the company is improperly leveraging its extensive customer base in one product area to capture customers for other products, thereby unfairly limiting competition. In other words, the charge is that Microsoft takes the aces won in one game and adds it to the new deck in the next game. If one company has 1 million customers for a product and undersells a new product to that existing customer base, another producer of the new product will be unable to gain access into the market. Under US law, when a new market develops, the playing field is supposed to start out even.[78]

The fitness landscape for personal computer programs now is changing. Change is being generated from at least three two points on the landscape. The obvious one is Intel's incessant drive to double computing speed every 18 months. Just as importantly, at the edges of the system exist experimenters. Diversity is still there, and shows up in the shareware market. This is the place for testing new software ideas, resulting in the

---

78 "The Force of an Idea" John Cassidy, The New Yorker Magazine, 1/12/98 ppgs. 32 - 37

development of such software as programs to un-install programs in Windows. Microsoft appears to follow a practice of integrating new software products into their primary operating system once they prove successful.

From that diversity emerged JAVA. JAVA is a new software language, which has the potential to make operating systems obsolete. Instead of individuals having operating systems, their computers can become like workstations relying on the programs that they interact with directly on the World Wide Web.

If Microsoft were to maintain its dependence on being a producer of operating systems, its life could become short lived if JAVA succeeds. That is why it is now trying to gain primacy in Internet inter-activity while producing its own version of JAVA. With its own version and its extensive distribution base, the company believes it has the power to successfully control the changing landscape. Unfortunately for Microsoft, the U.S. Justice Department feels that such an approach is predatory, which has led to the current anti-trust case against the company.

The ability to adapt to changing landscapes defines the true learning organization. Proof of the ability is recognized by a company's longevity and by demonstrations of adaptation and change over that time.

Conclusion

Maybe it is time to rewrite the story of Alice and the Cheshire Cat. When we last saw them, the Cheshire Cat was grinning from ear to ear, thinking he had tricked Alice. He told her it didn't matter which way she turned, if she did not know where she wanted to be.

When we have a vision about what is at the end of the trail, we will likely be surprised, and often disappointed. Columbus wanted to reach Cathay, not the Americas. In addition, Alice certainly didn't want to end up in the middle of a trial before the Queen of Hearts! In both cases, the need for adaptation was great—catastrophic in a sense.

With no vision, any trail has its challenges. These challenges can be met as they arise, instead of all at once. The trick is to emphasize finding energy sources, taking calculated chances, and going with the flow.

Chapter 7

The Complex Learning Organism

Quick adaptation is the only way to survive at the edge of chaos. Visions and long range planning are useless in a class 6 river.

Complex systems, ranging from autocatalytic (self-generating) compounds to the brain, all demonstrate the workings of the fundamental concepts described in Chapter 2. In fact, there is so much similarity between the processes associated with these apparently divergent systems that much of the corroborating theory for complex adaptive systems was developed independently within different disciplines. Only recently have scientists begun to recognize that they were looking at the same processes from different disciplines.

During the past fifteen years, organizational theory has generated comparable models from different perspectives. People were proposing different metaphors, which, we now know, actually demonstrated the same behaviors. The ecological, evolutionary, holographic, and quantum models of organization, for instance, have more in common than their proponents would like to admit. (Look at all the consulting money that would be lost if they admitted that their models were the same dressed up in different clothing!)

While it ultimately does not matter which of these examples is used as a metaphor for organizations, the emerging model of the brain currently has the greatest capacity for integrating these previously divergent ideas. We may now know more about how the brain functions then most other complex systems. Using strategies developed in complex systems research, scientists have successfully simulated how the brain functions -albeit at a much lower level of effectiveness than the human brain. With neural network systems machines have learned to recognize images and voices, to move independently of programming, to create professional quality art work, and most specifically, to learn without the direct involvement of humans. This research has been validated by identifying the existence of the same computational-like processes that are designed for these machines within chemo-electro-mechanical processes in animal and human brains.

The research enables us to draw a direct connection between how the brain functions and how we function in groups and organizations. There is, apparently, a self-similar relationship between the brain, organizations, and even society. We can identify these connections from a number of perspectives.

Consider a group of ants. The individual ant has a very, very small brain. Like all brains, the ant brain's primary function is to process information about change in its environment and to instruct the anatomical functions to perform their tasks in light of those changes. So it processes information coming through its senses, and acts on that information.

Some of the information, like the need to map out the direction to and acquiring new sources of food, is too complex for a single ant to process. In order for the ant to fulfill its primary mission of survival, it must process information and do work greater than it is capable of handling on its own. A larger information processing system emerges—the ant colony. That colony enables ants to reproduce and pass on genetic information—to survive—by being able to process more information than any individual ant can on its own. The colony develops into a small society. Members react to local stimuli following general rules. Nevertheless, the combined actions result in emergent coordinated behavior that produces the materials of survival. The colony is an expanded information processor, an expansion of the individual ant brains. The resulting behavior enables the ants' encoded genetic information to be passed on, even if the individual ant's own code is never reproduced.[79]

The ant colony is an extension of the ants' neural systems. Working together, ants perform the functions that enable ants, as a colony, to explore their environment and adapt as needed. The single human brain has evolved with the capacity to perform the same adaptive functions as an entire colony of ants (and then some, of course). The human brain is the individual's inherent tool for exploration and adaptation. While an ant colony is capable of and only needs to process a limited amount of information, human systems emerge as group brains capable of processing extensive amounts of complex information in response to the greater complexity of our lives.

Defining Learning

A number of disciplines with unpronounceable names, such as neurophysiology, are emerging to describe the various studies of brain functioning. The names are difficult because they represent the re-uniting of disciplines that were more distinct, resulting from the overlapping functions of complexity theory. At the same time, the research is only possible now thanks to the availability of the more sophisticated research equipment, including high speed supercomputers, computer-aided topography (CAT) scans, and electro-magnetic resonance imaging systems.

---

79 The complex life of ants is richly demonstrated in the computer program, SimAnt by Maxis. SimAnt was developed as an outgrowth early Artificial Life Conferences at the Santa Fe Institute.

The results of the research begin by describing the obvious: the brain's job is to receive and cause the body to react to outside stimuli with a response that allows the body to survive. In other words, the brain processes information to find energy that keeps the body fit. This is exactly what was earlier defined as the function of an organization.

If the environment were simple and static, the brain's job would be easy. Of course, this is not the case. The brain must react to stronger animals charging at apparently weaker animals, looking for its own meal of energy. It must also propel the animal to find new sources of energy when local energy sources run out. In reaction to all this, the brain's initial command is usually the simple choice of fight or flight. This and reproduction may be the only two behaviors that were hardwired into us at the start. But fight or flight proved to be inadequate for survival in our complex world. A more complex response emerged, called learning. As the scientist, Richard Restack explains:

"Successful adaptation to the environment requires that an organism be capable of learning"[80]

The standard dictionary definition of learning is that it is the acquisition of knowledge. Knowledge is the act of knowing, or having something firmly in one's memory.

This is the definition of learning used to describe most "learning organizations," Under this definition, an organization becomes a learning organization if it acquires information from other sources. Hence, to become a learning organization, writers propose setting up management development programs, executive study sessions, micro-worlds, and similar programs to acquire ever-increasing amounts of new information. "Steps to Becoming a Learning Organization" has been a boom to training programs throughout the US.

---

80 Restack, Richard. The Brain, p. 231

There is no sense of action upon the acquisition of knowledge in the traditional definition of learning. There seems to be an assumption that information acquisition will automatically lead to action.

In fact, as all trainers quickly learn, the acquisition of knowledge is no guarantee of action, let alone change. One of the greatest problems for trainers is that of transferability of training. Participants in training programs go back to their old jobs and continue acting as though nothing happened. Why? Because without concurrent changes in the student's environment, making a change can mean no longer fitting in with the current culture, resulting in the end of one's acceptance and employment. So, what do such trainees actually learn?

Take this idea one step further. Most organizations are in a never-ending quest for information. Thanks to the development of computers and the Internet, one of the biggest complaints is that we now receive too much information. If our organizations are acquiring so much knowledge why are they getting so bogged down?

The traditional definition of learning, it turns out, is short sighted. From a systems perspective, it only considers the inputs. There is no concern for results, and no recognition of the symbiotic relationship between a system, whether an individual or an organization, and its environment.

A more outcome-oriented definition of learning has emerged in complexity theory. As Restack explains it, learning is:

"...modifying behavior in response to experience"[81]

Restack's definition applies to all complex adaptive systems—it is the process of acquiring, processing, and reacting to complex information.

Under this definition, many systems can learn. Even viruses are capable of learning. This does not necessarily mean that the individual viral cell learns. The community of cells interacting with their host learns.

---

81 Restack, Richard. *The Brain.* p. 231

For instance, strains within a viral colony there co-exist primary and secondary strains of the virus. The secondary strains respond to different things than the predominant strain. The secondary strains are part of the virus's random repertoire of possibilities. When the environment changes, such as through the development of a vaccine, the door opens for one of the secondary strains to grow faster than the dominant strain, which has now lost its viral effectiveness. The secondary strain becomes dominant, we say the virus has mutated, and a new vaccine is needed. Under Restack's definition, the virus learned. Evolution is a learning process. *Adaptation is learning.*

We all have experiences where we acquire knowledge and don't learn. Ask a non-engineer/non-scientist who took calculus to define a function. S/he can't. Why? S/he never needed to use the information, so it never became new behavior. There was no learning.

An organization does not learn just by acquiring information. It only learns when it acquires and processes the information, and, if needed, changes its behavior because of that information. Later in the chapter we will compare how Ford learned as an organization in the 1980s, while General Motors was sitting, acquiring knowledge.

We see organizations change behavior all the time. They frequently change cultures, size, products, whatever the leader's vision requires for the moment. But that is not learning. Only behavior change that is in response to experience can be called learning—the only kind will insure survival of the organization.

In systems terms, a system is learning when it engages in a reinforcing feedback relationship with its environment. Or we could call it a mutual evolutionary cycle.

Chapter 2 described how changes between the market and automobile companies caused adaptation in the quality of cars. A similar example involves changes where technological developments start as add-ons, and eventually became standard equipment. Just consider some of the most visible automobile changes in the past forty years. Very few cars built in the 1950s and1960s included air conditioning or electronic locks and windows. The radios were the basic AM single speaker type. As the music industry changed, the radio changed with it—moving to 8 track tapes, cassette tapes, and now, compact disks. At each step, the new technology was first offered as an extra in a new car. Now, cars are equipped with stereo radios as standard equipment. While cassette decks are packaged as extras, they are bundled into sales packages that establish them as standard equipment. The same is true for air conditioning, and becoming true for electronic windows and locks.

These examples demonstrate that complex adaptive learning is not the result of long range planning. It is short term and incremental. It is emergent, growing out of the ongoing, co-evolutionary relationship between the system and its environment.

Learning does not have to be a conscious act, unless you want to assign consciousness to viruses. As such, it does not require leadership in the traditional sense. Consciousness can help, especially to improve the process of learning, because it allows us to understand the learning process itself. But learning more frequently acts as simply a response to a perceived need—an alteration in the environment.[82]

There have been a number of examples of good, unintended learning within the personal computer industry. Products that were invented with one use in mind, like word processing , evolved into entirely unintended markets, such as desktop publishing. The personal computer industry is filled with entrepreneurial companies with similar histories.

---

[82] One of the most important distinctions between human systems and others is our ability to learn about how we learn. This recursive process, which Chris Argyris calls "double loop learning," my be an exception within the complex systems world. Clearly, it enables humans to develop even more effective means of adaptation then our biological competitors. Applied to organizations, the ability to not only learn but to adjust how one's organization learns will greatly increase its competitiveness on a fitness landscape.

What a company must watch out for is dysfunctional learning. What is dysfunctional? In pop-psychology, the term is usually associated with family therapy and broken relationships. However, more often then not, the diagnosis is made from a value perspective instead of the originally intended systems perspective. Eventually, families were defined as dysfunctional if they did not fit the "Father Knows Best" model of parenting. This led to the false claim that the vast majority of families were dysfunctional in the 1980s.

The intended systems perspective of dysfunction in psychology was values neutral. The systems question psychologists meant to ask was whether the family was adapting in such a way as to enable the system to survive under adverse conditions, or in concert with changes in its environment. Considering that the environment of parenthood had drastically changed by the mid-1980s, with economic and social reasons resulting in dual-worker families, longer life spans leading to increased divorce levels, and other changes, there was no way that the mythical family of the 1950s could ever survive in our culture today.

The same holds true for organizations. We tend to look at our organizations from a values position instead of a systems perspective. Can we really say that a dysfunctional organization is one which doesn't have or varies from its vision, plan, product line, or budget? Or is it one that uses authoritarian management or stresses individualism instead of teams? The claim is not possible if the behavior fits the conditions of the environment.

Dysfunction appears when the system is no longer capable of staying in tune with changes in its environment. For instance, General Motors continued struggle to reinvent itself while it continued to lose market shares in the 1980s indicates the dysfunctional nature of its organizational system.

For a complex system, dysfunction leads to death, as we've seen with Digital Equipment Corporation and numerous entrepreneurial companies.

How the Brain Learns

Current models of the brain break its substance into two basic cellular components, neurons and synapses. Other brain matter appears to exist to enable the functioning of these two substances. The basic mechanical process relating neurons and synapses is the movement of chemo-electrical charges through the synapses to the billions of neurons.

The basic method for simulating and understanding the behavior of neurons and synapses is the computer process called a neural network. On a larger scale, neural networks are linked together in massive, parallel processing systems. The difference between how these systems work and the computer on your desk is like the difference between a clock and a beehive. Your computer can only perform tasks in sequence, and will not function without a programmer/creator/external mind establishing its instructions for action. On the other hand, a neural network has the capacity to start as a web of connections with no instructions. Over time it learns about its environment on its own, and acts according to its learning. In short, it is self-programming.

At the Beckman Institute of the University of Illinois, the Media Lab at the Massachusetts Institute of Technology, and elsewhere, un-programmed neural networks have been connected to robots of various types. The most popular is spider like. Watching the spider robot move is fun. Like a cartoon infant, it tends to stumble on obstacles—that is until it learns to identify the obstacles. Then the spider figures out how to get over or around the obstacles, without programming! *Data*, the humanoid robot in *Star Trek, The Next Generation*, is just a few generations ahead of these pioneers.

These machines learn much the same way as we do.

Our learning process starts with the neuron (or neurode in a neural network.). Each neuron has only one goal—to be excited.[83] [84] It wants to receive an electrical charge, and the more it gets the happier it is. The trouble is, all the neurons surrounding the individual one, also want the same thing. So there is a competition between autonomous agents acting from their own set of rules about how to get excited. The process is comparable to swarming described in chapter 6.

The synaptic connections are the bridges between the neurons through which the chemo-electrical charges flow. Synapses function in two ways. Some enable the charges to flow from one neuron to another. Others inhibit the flow. It is not too much of a reach as an analogy to think of enabling synaptic loops as reinforcing feedback, and inhibiting loops as balancing feedback.

The current flows when the system senses something. The electric spider senses its legs, and then its ability to move. The fetus senses nourishment or movement as the mother walks.

---

83 It probably feels strange to read about an inanimate object having a goal. During the 1940s, the study of cybernetics, demonstrated that all systems have inherent goals. Jeff Goldstein has pointed out, for example, a see-saw that has springs located at each end has a goal of achieving stability. Push on one side, and it bounces for a while till it comes to a stop.

84 The decision to be excited may be comparable to the need to acquire energy in self-organizing systems.

Figure 7-1: Baby hat and bowl

When something is really new, there is no recognition of what it is. The first time a baby sees a hat, there is no understanding of what it is. Yet, through the competition for the charge that is sent out, a pattern develops in the brain to represent the hat. Some neurons acquire a stronger charge than others. As the stimulus is repeated, patterns develop of alliances of neurons,—forming representations of the information that comes in through the senses. Eventually, the strength of these alliances makes it possible for us to quickly comprehend the outside world. After wearing the hat for a few weeks, the baby's brain has a strong representation of what it is. As patterns strengthen, they become the building blocks of more complex patterns of representation. At this point learning new information is achieved by associating the information with these higher order patterns, or by combining two or more patterns into a more complex representation. The more a given alliance is strengthened, the tougher it becomes to build new alliances.

Babies learn about hats well before they learn about bowls. The cute baby in our example, who grew up with lots of hats on his head, has just been introduced to his/her first bowl, with sticky, delectable applesauce in it. Guess what s/he does with it? [85]

The creation of patterns is the neural basis of the concept of paradigm that became so popular in the 1980s. A paradigm is a representation of the world that is so strong as to make invisible alternative representations. In short, the neuronal pattern has been strengthened so much that it takes a "whack on the side of the head" to bust loose.

Chaos is part of this learning process according to research on the volatility of brain waves.

Obviously, brain waves are flat when a person is dead. They also flatten out during an epileptic seizure. They are also found flatter in schizophrenics than in normal individuals. What is more surprising is that brain waives stay relatively flat when an individual experiences something that is known. In essence, the adult seeing the bowl expends very little energy recognizing that bowl. Conditions, under which adaptation—learning—is not at issue, are states close to equilibrium

Brain waves demonstrate swarming when there is learning by exhibiting chaos. That is, when a person is confronted with an unknown, the brain wave pattern appears random. When plotted in phase space, some researchers have demonstrated the possibility that there is a strange attractor within the brain dynamics.

However, when something is too outlandish—if the chaos is too strong—the information will just be rejected—there will be no association. Joel Barker demonstrates this situation in his video, *Discovering the Future: The Business of Paradigms*. He does a card trick where he

---

85 For a more complete description, see Minsky, Marvin. The Society of Mind, also Holland, Hidden Order

quickly turns over cards in a supposedly normal deck. There is one spade in the deck that is colored red, instead of black. But anyone reviewing the video perceives the spade to be black until the trick is shown slowly.

Barker's card trick demonstrates the thousands of times when we make such mistakes as when watching a magician. Only by slowing the process, by matching the low level of chaotic activity in the brain to our environmental experiences can we accept the paradigm (neural pattern) shift. Successful association, adaptation, requires a weak level chaos.

There are three kinds of learning—developmental, rote and associative. As we saw, developmental learning requires chaos. In a series of experiments with rats, William Greenough of the University of Illinois explored rote and associative learning. Greenough gave one group of rats aerobic type, repetitive exercises. (Can you picture the rats in their gym outfits!) This type of learning correlates with rote learning in schools. A second group was given problem solving exercises like climbing up on platforms and working through mazes.

Following a period of exercises, Greenough evaluated the synaptic change in the two groups. In the aerobic rats, he discovered that the synaptic connections strengthened, but there was not a clear cut increase in the number of connections. Doing the same thing repeatedly just made the rats better at doing that thing.

The second set of rats showed a marked increase in the number of connections, as a result of their problem solving activities. More connections mean a greater possibility of associations when confronting something new, resulting in a quicker recognition of the stimulus's newness. If IQ is defined as one's ability to solve complex problems (the more complex the higher the IQ), then we can say that the second group of rats experienced an increase in their IQ.[86]

---

86 Reported in Newsweek Magazine, February 19, 1996, p. 61

Greenough's research has important implications for any educational situation. It is not an indictment of rote learning. Basic responses need to be hardwired into us and reinforced. We do not want to have to think too long when we see a tiger coming after us in the wilds, or react to other experiences which are familiar. But to survive in a rapidly changing environment, such as the one experienced by modern organizations, we also need greater intelligence. To gain that, we need to spend more time experiencing problems rather than just responding the same old way.

Learning Organizations

The Chaos Exercise, described earlier, is very effective at simulating life in all kinds of organizations. More importantly, it has the ability to simulate chaos—both the pedestrian kind and the mathematical kind—in organizations.[87] After the game, and after the participants discuss the problems that caused chaos in the exercise, The participants are asked to list as many potential generators of chaos in their organizations as possible. At one regional food cooperative client, *Growmark, Inc.,* the group developed a list of 250 chaos generators in 15 minutes!

But the generators could not generate anything unless they were connected to other parts of the system. As the participants generated connection charts, patterns began to emerge. Most importantly, the whole image began to look like a neural network.

After evaluating the many systems that emerged from the exercise, I found I could group them into six primary meta-patterns that establish a good definition of any organization. These meta-patterns are:

---

[87] For a description of the mathematical *chaos that develops, see Guastello, Stephen, Chaos, Catastrophe, and Human Affairs.*

- **Technology:** the constellation of methods previously, currently, and potentially used to combine the raw materials of the organization into value-added commodities.
- **People:** the individuals and groups (ranging from the board of directors to the janitor) who were, are currently, or could potentially be involved in making the organization's product or service.
- **Market:** those individuals who consume, used to consume, or could consume the products and services.
- **Product:** the products or services that the organization provides, used to provide, or could provide.
- **Economy:** both the organization's internal health and the external economic and regulatory environment.
- **Eco-system:** the physical world as it impacts the organization and is impacted by the organization.

These six meta-patterns are composed of an infinite number of imbedded and inter-related systemic connections. The relationships are defined by both balancing and reinforcing feedback loops, change continually, and represent the functioning of the total organization (Figure 7-2: The Complex Organization).

Two important concepts stand out when viewing this list. First is its use of time. Most planning is limited by a look at the present projected into the future. The organization takes a snapshot of itself and plans based upon this slice of life image.

The definitions of the meta-patterns serve to establish more of a motion picture view of the organization. This is very important because, as the case study of Honda Motor Corp will demonstrate, complex systems are, to some extent, bound by their past. Past policies, beliefs, equipment, etc. create limits on what can be done now or in the future.

Second is the apparent loss of traditional organizational boundaries. The old we/they thinking placed the market, external economy, and especially the ecological world outside the boundaries of the organizations. Here we see that they both impact and are impacted by the internal systems. The least considered block, the Eco-system, provides the best example. On the one hand, as California businesses know, a sudden, major change in the Eco-system, such as an earthquake, will change how the company does business. Smaller changes, like the long-term use of resources, also causes change. And the organization sends products into the Eco-system which need disposal, changing that system as well.

Boundaries do emerge in this system. The boundaries include what does not currently fit into a particular organization's system. For instance, individuals living in Miami may be outside of the market boundary of a mom and pop clothing store in Seattle. But like the edges of a fractal image, even these boundaries are poorly defined and permeable. Once the store lists their products on the World Wide Web, the market boundaries become international. More importantly, much learning starts with change at the boundaries (association) that are later imported into the organization. So the boundaries, themselves, always change. When unencumbered by a controlling vision, they organize and reorganize, as conditions require.

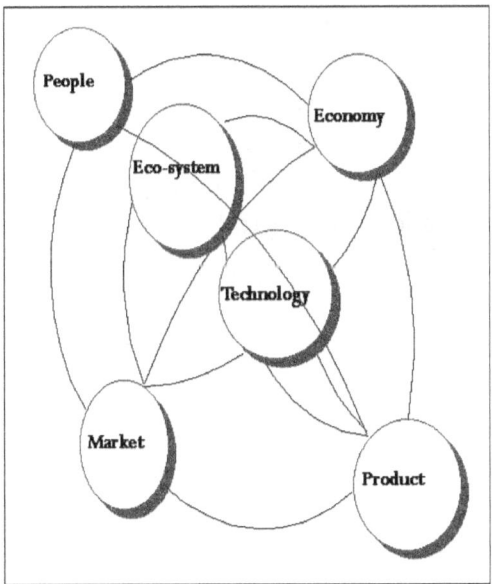

Figure 7-2: The Complex Organization

Mapping Meta-patterns

Mapping relationships at this meta-pattern level gives a very good description of the current "paradigm" of an organization—the schema that defines how the organization currently understands its world. Just as we can demonstrate that a neural network has learned by identifying changes in its neural patterns, learning can be demonstrated in an organization by identifying changes in a particular organization's model.

As an example, compare the well-publicized histories of three automobile companies, General Motors, Ford, and Honda.

Ford and General Motors long time schema was represented by a relationship between technology, product, and the market place. Changes in technology lead to creation of new products, which the companies hoped, would change the market place. The internal combustion engine was packaged into a buggy, making the Model T Ford.

The basic schema (Figure 7-3) was that over time, technology changed the product, which changed the marketplace. All feedback was reinforcing but unidirectional.

The schema stayed in place at Ford, GM, and Chrysler for a half century. At first, Ford's schema was even stronger then GM's, since Ford originally failed to respond to a changing market place by adding color to their cars. Nevertheless, for a half century, the basic process was, create new technology, add it to the product, and sell it to the market.

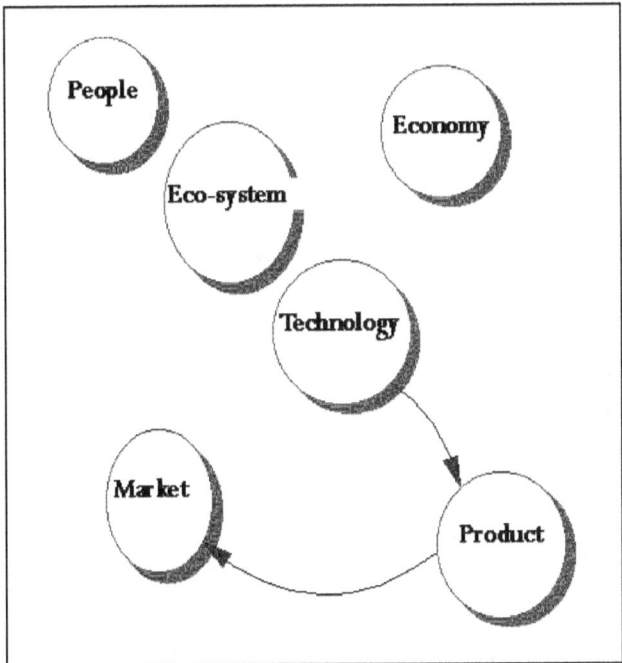

Figure 7-3: The Automobile Industry Learning Model

By the way, this schema appears to represent the entrepreneurial stage of many technology companies. When I showed the case history to people at Digital, there was an immediate recognition of their own situation. Since then, numerous people have recognized the schema in their entrepreneurial experiences. A new or better mousetrap is invented and sold to the market. Sometimes it sells. However, if the market is not interested, as is often the case, the company dies.

In the 1970s, there was a major change in the automobile market meta-pattern. It was caused by many factors including the oil embargo and increased price of oil, high inflation, and new entrants into the competition—the Japanese and Europeans.

By 1980, crises had developed. Chrysler almost went bankrupt, and Ford and GM were quickly losing market share. A response was needed.

General Motors and Chrysler apparently followed their same old, tried and true formula. They used technological changes, in this case cost cutting reductions, to catch up to the market place. The GM J car and the Chrysler K car were designed as the first major response to the Japanese. Both were smaller, boxier, and more stripped down, to allow competition based on price.

Ford had a better idea. First, the company brought in and let lose a bunch of consultants. According to Nancy Badore, a Human Resource Development executive at Ford during the transition, the company really had no idea what it was doing at that time.[88] We could say that the company instituted some chaos—a bunch of little experiments that allowed swarming to begin.

Eventually, the idea of "Quality is Job 1" evolved into a realignment of the building blocks as Deming-style experiments developed throughout the company with replication reinforcing their success. That is, a few quality experiments worked and were iterated into larger experiments until they became the dominant schema of the company. The process finally established the people of Ford as more than part of the technological process, their minds were engaged as well. The schema connected the people with both the technology and the product subsystems. (Figure 7-4)

---

[88] From a presentation by Dr. Nancy Badore at the 1990 conference of the Organization Development Network.

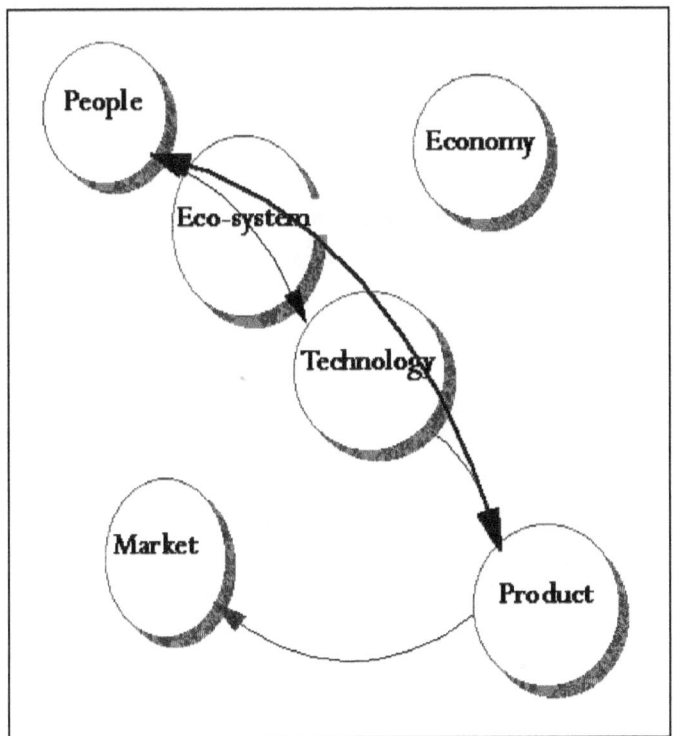

Figure 7-4: Ford's Quality is Job 1

Learning didn't stop there. It came time to develop the first Taurus. The first step in this well documented process was one of two critical steps that finally transformed Ford's schema. The design team broke down the walls (subsystems) within the People meta-pattern—cross-functional design teams were used. A second critical barrier was also broken. The design teams decided that to effectively design a new product, they needed a better understanding of what the market wanted. So cross discipline teams went out and held focus meetings, interviews, and surveys of potential buyers and incorporated their findings into the final design. In other words, a final reinforcing feedback connection developed between the Market and the People meta-patterns (Figure 7-5). This learning was what lead to Ford's success.

But neither the success nor the learning was continuous. In 1989, Ford moved into another period of financial crises. While riding a wave of success, it had to lay off thousands. The reason, in 1989 the country moved into a recession. As Figure 7-5 shows, there were no connections with the Economic meta-pattern. Ford had no early warning of the impending slump, and had to adapt under more difficult circumstances than may have occurred with more forewarning.

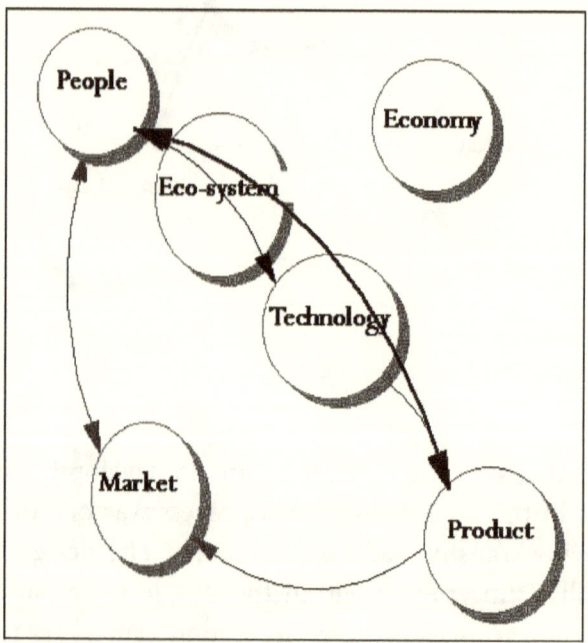

Figure 7-5: Ford's Better Idea

The Ford story shows what learning really is in an organization. If we consider the meta-patterns as neurons (and actually representative of an infinite number of smaller relationships whose connections are also always competing for excitement), then learning is the ability to adapt the network over time in response to experience.

To switch to quality management, to re-engineer, to change one's culture may or may not be true organizational learning. Does the change fit the flow of change within the organization's larger system? Or is it an attempt to change without consideration of the true needs of the organization to survive.

While Ford appeared to have stopped learning, its new schema did position it to come out of the recession in early 1990 in the lead. Taurus continued to be the best selling car in its class. But the company is now returning to its old, dysfunctional ways. In the redesign of the 1997 Taurus, it has been reported that top management actually overruled design decisions made by the design team (such as the placement of the side mirror). The new model's market share slipped behind the Toyota Camary. This reversion back to the leader-drive technology to product change demonstrates how easy it is to forget new learning when it has not been reinforced.

Searching for Fitness

By the early 1990s, Ford had developed a sense of fitness relative to its system. Such fitness depends upon whether the change is in line with the organization's needs at that point in time. *Fitness exists when an organization's process is in line with those required of the system at a given point in time to enable its survival.*

An organization's fitness is understood by exploring the current schema, both as it exists and by identifying what is not being responded to at a given point in time. When something is changing and there is no response, such as changes in the economy not being identified, then there is a problem. The definition of a problem can be restated as: *a problem exits when there is a difference between the demand of different parts of the system and what the system is doing.* Of course, this will be the case most of the time in any complex organization. Responding to it effectively is the key to long term survival.

Deming's proposal for continuous improvement, even continuous learning, provides a major step towards a systemic resolution of problems in a learning organization. However, at least in the way it is applied, it stops short of establishing a true learning organization. As the Ford story demonstrates, an organization cannot just be concerned with quality—the connection between people, product, technology and the market place. Instead, the learning organization must be capable of continually changing its schema based on its identification of problems and adaptation of its purpose.

Learning, the never-ending quest for fitness, must replace the goal of quality for an organization to survive in the white water. Changing the organization's schema never stops in the learning organization. The catch is, even if we think it stopped, it goes on without us, with the likely result of tripping us up.

Honda's move away from employee participation in 1993 is a good example of the possible problems that result when the organization stops learning. In 1993, Nobuhiko Kawamoto, the new chairman of Honda, decided that the heavy reliance on employee participation was slowing the company down, resulting in its loss of market share. To make Honda more agile and responsive to changing market whims, Kawamoto decided to centralize some decision making at Honda.[89]

A look into Honda's history, and development of the meta-pattern diagram (Figure 7-6) demonstrates that Honda's problems emanated from a totally different, systemic problem.

---

89 "A Car is Born", *Business Week Magazine* (9/13/93)

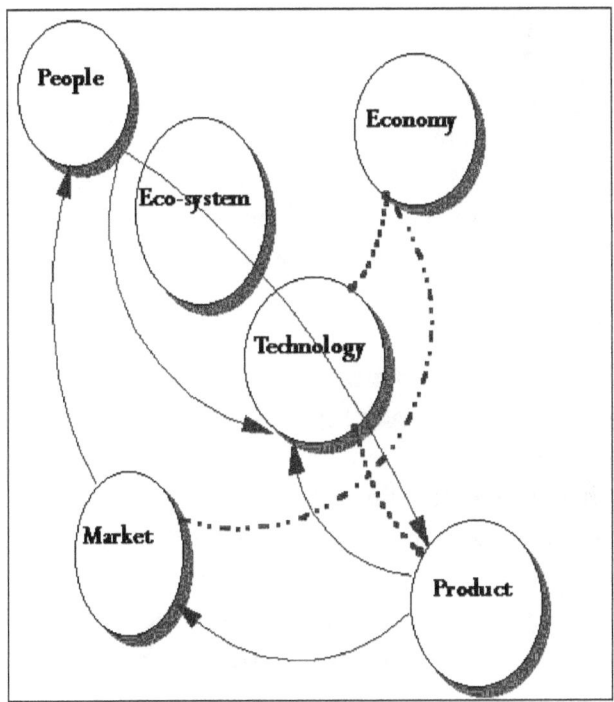

Figure 7-6: The Honda Way

Honda's success came first from its Civic and then Accord models. These cars fit the needs of the growing US baby boomer population in the 1970's and early 1980's—young, single or newly married, moderate-income individuals wanting engineering quality at an affordable price. They were the largest group of consumers, and they brought Honda's capacity to full production.[90]

At that time, Accords were sold at premium prices. Going to a Honda dealership (according to the Post article and my experience) was like

90 The Washington Post (10/3/93)

going to a ComputerLand store. In the sales person's mind you were there because you already knew what you wanted, and you did not expect any special deals.

During the mid-eighties, the market changed. Ford came out with the Taurus, a competitively priced, slightly larger, American car with quality engineering and a new style. The Taurus cut into the aging, married baby boomer group market. Some baby boomers began having babies. These former Honda owners bought the 1980's version of the station wagon—the Dodge Mini-van.

In the late 1980s, the Japanese economy began to slow while the US economy went into a recession followed by a slow recovery.

During this time, based on its success in sales and management, Honda's schema changed little. It added the Prelude line, (another coupe sedan), a failed Accord wagon, and minor styling changes. It also moved manufacturing of Accords to the US.

By 1991, a problem, based on our definition, clearly existed. The analysis demonstrates differences in the market and economy (and probably in available technology, too) meta-patterns with no change in product, people, or used technology by Honda.

Two dynamics converged to bring about the problem.

The first dynamic supported the thesis that rote learning only strengthens the synaptic connections, at least at the superficial level. What Honda's history demonstrated was first recognized by Peters, that companies keep doing what they tend to do well, even after the market has long changed. In systems terminology, positive reinforcement breeds balancing feedback.

In the same way as rote learning fosters strengthened synaptic connections, behaviorists consistently demonstrate that a person will continue doing something for which s/he has been consistently rewarded long after the reward is taken away. In fact, we can think of this as a habit. When a habit forms, it is difficult to recognize when the habit becomes destructive. The habit insulates the individual from the potential effects of changes in one's environment. Heroin addicts start getting high to escape the chaos of their ever-changing environment. As the drug quickly reaches dangerous levels, the addict fails to recognize the danger, and continues the habit, frequently till death. This dampening of information regarding change is, as described before, the nature of balancing feedback.

In neural network terms, the pattern is being continually reinforced until it becomes difficult for other neurons to successfully compete for stimulation.

Honda's case demonstrates the effect of such habit making in organizations. Honda continued to sell over 360,000 Accords a year, even as they lost market share. That's positive reinforcement!

The second dynamic operating was in the technology meta-pattern. Technology decisions made a number of years back returned to limit Honda's ability to adapt. In this case it was the manufacturing plant's physical structure that dampened Honda's ability to change. According to the Post article, even though Honda considered developing a mini-van, the company's manufacturing plants were not built tall enough to accommodate the vehicle. Their plants were designed for building small to midsize sedans.

Honda's technology problem demonstrates the function of determinism within a complex system. In linear systems, determinism enables the predictability of the future. Given starting point A and direction B, the future will eventually reach predictable point C. In complex, chaotic systems, a system's outcome is also defined by the starting condition, unless a random act changes the direction. But the outcome is unpredictable because the starting condition cannot be re-identified. At the same time, determinism helps establish the boundaries within which the system can operate.

Honda's ability to adapt to the market change was limited by the boundaries established by technological decisions at the starting point. Mini-vans fell outside that boundary.

The reason for reviewing this technological issue is simple. Honda's problem was not in its people meta-pattern. Even with the best management of one part of the system, the ability to adapt can be thwarted by unexpected impacts from other parts of the system. As many entrepreneurs learned in the 1980s, the best people programs do not guarantee success, nor does the best technology, financing, quality, or what ever. In Honda's case, although the results could not be predicted, without a major intervention in technology, the company's position was doomed from the start.

As with many Japanese companies, Honda is highly diversified. Consequently, lower sales in one area are easily made up in other areas. This gave Honda plenty of time to retool and develop a vehicle that could compete with the Ford Taurus and the surging Nissan vehicles. By 1998, with the release of a new Accord, Honda automobile sales were again soaring in the U.S., although the competition against Ford and the Pontiac Grand Prix was getting tighter.

Applying Learning Theory

One way to assess an organization's fitness is through an exercise that identifies changes going on in and between the six meta-patterns. Such an exercise is an outgrowth and extension of the micro-worlds systems exercises used by Senge.

A review of the Ford case gives some idea of how this process works. As you will recall, the case identified that the final paradigm at Ford connected the People, Technology, Product, and Market fitness landscapes in a large reinforcing feedback loop. At the same time, it identified that the economy fitness landscape was changing rapidly, yet there was no connection from that pattern to the rest of the system. Things went out of whack because of the disconnection.

From this analysis, we can say that Ford's fitness strategy needed to include a way in which changes in the economy could be linked to the other changes in the organizational system. Once this fitness strategy is identified, it is possible to establish short-term goals and objectives that can achieve this end.

The actual planning process is chaotic in itself. It involves

- Identifying what change is happening in each of the fitness landscapes;
- Whether the change will cause changes in the other landscapes (reinforcing feedback) or is controlling change elsewhere in the system (balancing feedback);
- Showing the connections that do exist;
- Assessing from a very chaotic looking map the major landscape interactions;
- Determining where change is being controlled that needs to be reinforced, where it is being reinforced and may need controlling (if possible) and where change needs to be connected in some way with the rest of the system;

One very revealing application of this process was facilitated at the NASA Lewis Research Center in 1993. Before doing the exercise, the Center's managers described their purpose as developing new technologies and finding ways to transfer those technologies into the private sector. On the day the session was conducted, everyone at the Center was holding their breath to find out if Congress was going to continue the Space Station Freedom program. One of the things, which the managers wondered about, was why they kept running into funding problems such as that being encountered by the Space Station.

During the exercise, the participants agreed that changes in the economy had led to major changes in the priorities of the electorate. This, in turn, helped determine their funding (the market). Even as they were changing technology for everyone else, they were not receiving the funds needed to change their own technology. The market place also changed with the development of well-funded competitors including nationally run programs in other countries (France and Japan for instance) and in the private sector.

The Center's fitness plan began to read something like, "Changes in the economy and market place are limiting our ability to create new technology rapidly enough to compete in the market place. This is also leading to a loss of personnel, which is also resulting in slowing down our ability to continue to develop new technologies."

The organization most responsible for developing new technologies was being restricted from creating those technologies by the weight of its own system!" It was obvious from this fitness review that the Center had to take actions which would change some of the feedback links from controlling to reinforcing, if it was to survive.

Learning Organisms Must Forget

Honda was unable to adapt because it had difficulty forgetting. Deep within its technological neurons dwelled the memory of building sedans, which existed physically in terms of the ceiling size of the production facility. To overcome the problem, Honda needed to build new connections, new knowledge. This could be done in various ways, such as outsourcing production to another company, Honda's short-term solution, or building a new plant with higher ceilings, which it has now done.

Memory in a complex system is the deterministic nature of the system. The future status of complex systems are established at their starting point, just as with linear systems. Only in complex systems, the outcomes are unpredictable. Honda's production facilities represented a memory that acted unpredictably, holding the organization back from making a critical adaptation.

Learning requires the ability to disrupt, but not destroy the deterministic line. This is the ability to forget. This is essential when on a path going in the wrong direction.

Poet and songwriter Paul Simon gave an example of such learning as his personal creative process in an interview with David Frost on April 10, 1970. In the interview, Simon was explaining how he wrote the song, *Bridge Over Troubled Waters*. Frost asked him to describe how he knew when one idea was not working. Simon replied, "When I go there and it is not where I want to be." If Simon cannot get a path *out of his mind*, he stagnates on the song.

Neural network researchers have confirmed that the ability to forget is critical to the process of learning. According to Maureen Caudill and Charles Butler:

> "…we [also] want the system to respond to an environment that changes over time. If the environment can change, the responses appropriate to a particular stimulus can also change. If we do not permit the system to forget, it will be difficult to retain it to a new, more appropriate behavior when circumstances change."[91]

General Motors has difficulty changing partly because its history—memory—is so long. Its production facilities, technology, and management have followed a single path for a period of over 70 years. The Japanese automakers were faced with a shorter memory when faced with the challenges of oil shortages in the 1970s. Because they had less to forget, they were capable of responding much faster to market changes. It is understandable that General Motors saw the best way out as eventually dumping the old system by creating a new, disconnected system unencumbered with GM's memory. The result was creation of the Saturn line.

---

91 Caudill, Marueen and Butler, Charles: *Naturally Intelligent Systems.*

Maintaining an adaptable system, a system on the edge of chaos, is much more viable in the long run as demonstrated by Honda's eventual renewal under Kawamoto. However, forgetting is not that easy. GM hoped to birth Saturn in such a way as to leave it unaffected by GM's history. That never happened. Within a year after the announcement of the new company, there already were reports of how GM management was cutting Saturn's development budget and forcing it to conform to the use of some of GM's materials and resources.

Saturn's current success may actually be a result of this problem. Forgetting must be balanced with memory to insure survival. When an organization's environment changes, there is a tendency to "throw out the old and start with the new." There are massive layoffs, hiring of a new CEO and management staff. It is like killing the organization and birthing a new one in its spot.

Such cataclysmic change results in a total loss of memory—resources—which have benefited to the organization. The amnesia includes losing the basic skills of survival. The organization must start learning from the beginning, as if it was a baby all over again learning to again walk and talk. The loss in time, energy, and resources can be more damaging in the end to a larger, complex organization, than developing the type of glitch that Honda faced.

Conclusion

Various complex adaptive systems all demonstrate a basic group of behaviors, which allows them to gain information from the environment, adapt, and then export new information into the environment. They are all involved in a dance of development and learning, of moving from the less complex to the more complex, searching for better fitness with the changing environment. Other phenomenon that demonstrate this behavior include organisms which develop from single cells based on the complex interactions with the DNA molecule, an ecological niche, a beehive or ant hill, and even the evolution of science, itself.

Others have used these different systems as metaphors for their organizational theory. To some extent, we are all speaking the same language. The essential distinction is whether the metaphor correctly demonstrates an understanding of the underlying science of complex systems, or whether the author has jumped from the words used by the scientists into some land of magic.

The most important point is to understand that adaptation—learning—is more of a natural, unguided process than previously believed. This is not a matter of magic. Self-organization generates the learning process. Sometimes it is only as Monday morning quarterbacks that we can easily look back and say, "Oh, that's why it works!"

The danger is trying too hard to tame this process. As humans our greatest amount of learning is done in an unscheduled, playful environment—between the ages of birth till about four years of age. But we are constantly reading our environment and adapting to its needs.

Organizations have the habit of working in reverse. Modern organizations and their leaders try to impose their wills on their surroundings. As the allusions to Digital to demonstrate, this is a formula for failure, for it fails to allow learning in response to the rapid changes in one's surroundings.

Chapter 8

Leadership and Learning Organisms

Science observes nature to discover connections and patterns. Scientists, whether shamans or astrophysicists, have shared, until recently, the ultimate goal of helping humankind control the forces of nature. Such control would make us like gods, providing safety and, ultimately, immortality.[92]

The first two creation stories described in Chapter 1 were the result of scientific investigations in older times. Both expressed a possibility of achieving the goal of control. The first described the goal in blatant terms, it was the responsibility of humankind to dominate and subdue the earth. The second was subtler. It suggested that control would be found within the self. Personal control would allow one to see through the illusion of temporal connections, leading to unity with the true whole.

As science moved into the modern age, its observations led more and more scientists to conclude that a complete understanding and control of nature is impossible. To achieve such a goal would require knowing the exact nature of the starting conditions. This, it was recognized, would be impossible. Without the potential for control, the vision of

---

92 *The Art of Magic,* PBS Television, 1998

domination vanished. Humankind finally became a part of nature, not the centerpiece within a much larger domain.

Throughout this book, we have tried to apply new scientific learning to strategic organizational issues. It is now time for the final test. What do the discoveries in science say about the nature of leadership, especially when leadership, itself, is so closely tied to the notion of domination.

To begin with, take a second look at the three creation stories in the first chapter.

The first composite creation story developed in landed cultures such as Babylon. These cultures created the first city-states. They valued centralization of power, and applications of that power to win wars and build massive architectural structures. The stories from these cultures identify nature as the chaos that must be defeated, so that humankind could control the earth. The first creation story established the role of leaders as Conquerors.

The second creation story came from cultures whose environment made them dependent upon cycles of time. This dependency could have resulted from cycling through a group of hunting sites throughout the year, from developing an agrarian calendar dependent upon the seasons, or from the cycles of high and low water along a major river such as the Ganges River.

Cultures whose thinking is dominated by the second creation story have less of a history of development in the modern sense. They are more likely to be subjugated by dominating cultures. Yet within this worldview, subjugation does not matter. Those with a cyclical worldview are more patient with nature, believing that the cycles of time will bring back the herds and the water. Tending the fields at the right time is the critical issue. Chaos is a temporary condition to live through before rebirth in the cycle of time. The second creation story established the role of leaders as Stewards.

The new creation story of science establishes that change is continuous, unpredictable, and uncontrollable. Time flows with space in curving directions from the past to the future. What is ahead can be seen for only a short distance, the future is always new and unexplored. The new creation story establishes the leader as an Explorer.

What dimensions define the new leader, the Explorer? Chapters 3 and 4 discussed the critical issue of sight, demonstrating that Holsight, rather than vision or hindsight, is critical to survive in a fast changing environment. Chapter 5 and 6 discussed the organization's application of chaos to the organization's ability to change and survive on the white water. Chapter 7 discussed the learning process and the nature of memory as central to the ability to adapt in a changing environment.

These three dimensions, the use of sight, chaos, and memory, are central to the process of leadership in the new organization. To understand their roles, they will be described in each of the three leadership styles.

	Conqueror	Steward	Explorer
Use of Sight	Foresight	Hindsight	Holsight
Use of Chaos	Strong chaos	Strong control	Weak chaos
Use of Memory	Destroys memory	Remembers everything	Remembers and forgets

Figure 8-1: Leadership Differences

The Conqueror

Conquerors use foresight. They place their hopes on what they can build for the future. Conquerors spend their time looking ahead, beyond, into the distance of time. Conquerors are also farsighted, they often miss what is right in front of their noses. Conquerors stress the big picture, the ends. They do not concern themselves with the details, with the means.

The great conquerors included Ghengis Khan, William the Conqueror, and Ponce de Leon. They were men and a few women who took control of their surroundings, building their vision of society while eliminating existing civilizations.

People are seduced into following leaders with foresight. The vision provides hope for a future in a world that appears uncivilized, chaotic. Conquerors exhibit congruence, they "walk the talk," at least on the surface. The seduction leads to alignment, a by-product of this relationship. Those who work most closely with the Conqueror happily fulfill the needs of the leader.

Of the two traditional leadership types, the Conqueror appears more charismatic. His/her charisma reinforces significant psychological baggage that comes with charisma, including narcissistic behavior, follower dependency, and loss of will in the follower. Observed from the outside, the difference between a David Koresh of the Branch Davidians and a Stephen Jobs is only a matter of degrees. But none of the popular leadership literature has taken note of this relationship.

Because of the charisma, Conquerors never have a problem gaining at least an entourage of followers. There are always a few insecure individuals around who are looking for any father figure to provide them with a sense of security. The leader's confidence in the future that the leader plans to create acts as a magnet for others. Such leaders appear extroverted and highly energetic in public. The spirit is very contagious. Those close by hold on like fly paper. They reinforce the Conqueror's confidence. A reinforcing feedback loop develops, which leads to ignorance of other changes which may be developing in the system.

Conquerors replace organizational memory with new meaning. "Destruction is cool." Nothing learned in the past is valued. Conquerors break the stone tablets of the conquered and execute the high priests. They break up family groups (divide and conquer) through restructuring, and force the conquered to bow down to them or their gods, foregoing all that went before. Che Guevarra's preaching "revolution for revolution's sake" and Mao Tse Tong with his Cultural Revolution of the 1960s, were trademarks of successful Conquerors.

In modern organizations, Conquerors, like Stephen Jobs, Bill Gates, or Stephen Wolfram tend to start new organizations where they can benignly create new memory. Building a new culture around a vision is effective for an entrepreneurial organization in the short run. It pulls people and systems together quickly. So long as the organization is single-dimensional, such as having only one product line, this management style works.

What happens underneath is creation of an organization at equilibrium. The level of complexity is low because the entrepreneur is creating her own technology, product and market. For most such organizations, success is not the result of the culture or vision. It comes from the organization being lucky enough to be sucked into a niche that enables it to grow. For Conqueror led organizations, problems develop later, when the organization is more complex requiring the organization to function at the edge of chaos. Then it must face the struggle of building in weak chaos. Otherwise, like Digital, it dies.

When the Conqueror perishes on an expedition, often the whole crew perishes with him/her. When the entrepreneurial founder of an organization dies or leaves the organization, the organization, likewise, has great difficulty adjusting. One client has explained the problem as having to try to replace the 600-pound gorilla (who can sit anywhere he wants) and not being certain whether he should be replaced. The loss creates a decision making vacuum just when the organization is finally faced with confronting the complex, ever changing nature of the real world. Sometimes it is easier to catch onto an imaginary space ship behind a comet then to suddenly face reality.

Dependency is a critical reason why many founder-led companies fail to survive following the loss of the foresighted founder. Once the leader is gone, the sense of security is gone and the congruence is broken. The vision of the future is gone, and memory of how to go back, if that were possible, has been destroyed. The followers are faced with competing interpretations provided by individuals who have not demonstrated their comparable success.

One strategy used for replacing the founder is to hire another Conqueror. Conquerors are frequently installed in turn-around situations because of their well-publicized history of success. This may work in the short term in turn around situations, but it becomes dangerous when the new Conqueror comes into an existing organization and attempts to transform it to his/her vision.

Installing Conquerors into existing organizations is also a favorite approach of many venture capitalists, most of whom are, themselves Conquerors. Frank Lorenzo, who bought Continental Airlines and ran it into bankruptcy, demonstrates the problem. Ross Perot's inability to translate his success as an entrepreneurial conqueror at EDS into the political arena not only demonstrates the problems, but also shows how the success comes from something other than the entrepreneurial model of leadership.

When a Conqueror is brought into an equilibrium organization, the entire management team is dismissed or cornered so as to become ineffective. A we/they attitude often develops between the new management team and those who see their own salvation in support of that team verses the carriers of the organization's history. To bring about the transformation, there is a period of high activity as a new culture is inserted through intensive training programs. Everyone is indoctrinated into the new vision. No wonder some people feel like the company is trying to initiate them into a new religion.

Of course this is really the problem of instilling large change into an equilibrium organization. The results of this approach, as discussed in Chapter 5, are to reject the invasion. The result is usually deadly to both sides.

An alternative strategy is to merge the leaderless organization into an already institutionalized company, or some other choice of death. If the merger works, the choice is not really death. In his book, *Complexity: Life at the Edge of Chaos*, Roger Lewin describes how, even after death, artifacts of a previously living entity continue to interact with and affect the environment. This is not a new age concept of reincarnation or of the universal soul. It represents a purely physical reality of the relationships within systems [93]

Probably the most frequently used strategy to replace Conquerors is to replace the Conqueror with a hindsighted leader—a Steward—who is well versed in the visionary's doctrine. The strategy maintains the status quo and rebuilds a sense of security. It also reinforces the state of equilibrium within the organization.

The Conqueror is a great lover of chaos—strong chaos. Any battle to take over space is chaotic at its core, even when broad strategies such as flanking are used. On the battlefield, determining which foot soldiers live or die results from a random set of events. The organizational Conqueror attempts to simulate this experience in the workplace by instilling chaos in his/her troops every chance possible.

CEOs brought me in to a number of companies wanting me to teach his or her staff about chaos theory. Each hoped that, following my

---

93 See Michaels, Mark, " Thoughts on the 25th Anniversary of the Organization Development Institute," *The Organization Development Journal*, Vol. 11(2) pgs 51 - 56 for a discussion of how this concept of dissipation is applied to the profession of Organization Development.

instruction, his followers would understand the reason behind his apparent madness. In one such company, staff explained to me that the CEO's modis operendi was to always shake things up. The company frequently reorganized, and the CEO frequently changed decisions or made new ones based on what he just learned at a conference.

When this happens, followers become tired of keeping up with the CEO. Because priorities keep changing, there is never closure on a project. Followers burn out quickly leading to high turnover rates, which reinforce the elimination of past memory.

Although a number of management gurus such as Peters[94] have supported this chaotic philosophy, when experienced from below, it becomes obvious that this is no way to run a company. As discussed in Chapter 5, when there is strong chaos, followers tend to give up and follow another leader.

Thousands of leaders followed the strategies prescribed for Conquerors in the entrepreneurial literature. For some previously inexplicit reason, they failed to reach star status. So long as the system's purpose is not congruent with the vision, the rate of attraction quickly fades the further one gets from the visionary. Support ebbs quickly. It is not possible to bring an organizational purpose into line with a personal vision. Success follows the demands of the system, not the individual.

Conqueror's can be dumped just as quickly as their meteoric rise to stardom once the vision goes sour. When a Digital or Sun Microsystems begins to fail the Conqueror is deserted. Those caught up in the system hope that a successor will quickly discover the right path. Digital's founder, Ken Olsen, is still pursuing his vision of centralized computing at a small entrepreneurial company, Advanced Modular Solutions. Steve Jobs attempted to renew his vision with the creation of the NeXt computer with little success. He appeared to set aside his vision when,

---

94 Peters, Tom, *Thriving on Chaos*

after returning to Apple in 1997, he announced a deal with Microsoft to a chorus of loud boo's from his ardent supporters. The visionary leaders of the early 1980s have disappeared from the scene. Is leadership supposed to be so transitory?

Stewards

Stewards rule as a privilege of divine right. In other words, the authority of their rule comes from history. This makes Stewards hindsighted. Their vision is drawn from the history of their experiences. George Bush had a vision, regardless of pronouncements to the contrary. His vision was one of a world kept at peace through the strength of the US military making it possible for the U.S. to import his perception of its value system. The value structure incorporated an interrelationship between self-determination, a free market place, and minimal federal involvement in local issues. There was nothing new to George Bush's vision. It came directly from the economic conservatism that developed in the Republican party during the 1980s.

Bush's claim to the presidency was that it was his turn. His role as Vice President gave him the right to be Reagan's successor. However, the country saw that history was not addressing newly emerging issues and, after four years, dumped the successor. (Bob Dole had the same problem, believing that his position in the Republican Party gave him the right to be the Republican leader. His hindsight also led him to misread the changes in the moral landscape which, had it been 20 years earlier, would have assured a victory for him.)

Stewards frequently replace successful Conquerors who have moved on to better or different pastures. Ronald Reagan looked into the future and created a vision of smaller government. His vision and methods demonstrate the clear markings of a Conqueror. George Bush followed as one of our country's Stewards. The Steward's strength in this setting is his ability to identify, understand, and translate the founder's vision. By doing so, the Steward maintains the sense of security and stability established by the farsighted, charismatic leader. The ship of state supposedly stays on course.

Steward led organizations operate in maintenance mode, repeating what's worked before. Organizations under their command become more departmentalized and complex as the vision is institutionalized and systems develop to protect the vision's role within the group. Production systems and technology are set. The primary market is established. If the organization is growing before the Steward comes on board, then its growth spurt ends and the organization's processes become institutionalized. The Steward fights to hold everything together.

Stewards are as nearsighted as Conquerors are farsighted. Stewards have difficulty seeing changes coming up ahead on the path.

There is nothing glorious about being a Steward, so they rarely stand out in their leadership capacity. They do not become the stars of management theorists. Sometimes, like Shakespeare's King Lear or General Motors' Roger Stemple, those professing conquest give them a sort of clownish figure. In Stemple's case, his fame came at the hands of a Steward killer, Michael Moore, who created the movie, *Roger and Me*. Otherwise, Stemple avoided the limelight. He never wrote an autobiography and his name rarely appears in the leadership literature.

Stewards venerate memory as their way of validating their leadership. Organizational Stewards emphasize using tried and true strategies to continue existing success. The condition which Peters and others have correctly identified, in which the organization just keeps on doing what it was doing successfully, is the order of the day.

Followers work in awe of Stewards. This is not the same as charisma. Rather than drawing people to them through high energy and the challenge of the quest, Stewards seduce and hypnotize their followers into a false sense of security by glorifying the past. By following the past, followers feel confident about the decisions they make, because the choices worked in the past.

There is a great sense of security working for a hindsighted leader. Fear of the unknown future is replaced with the stability of the known, the memory of the past. A sense develops that the system is working fine. Real change disappears. The future feels secure. Complacency settles in. The organization exhibits either cyclical behavior or rests at equilibrium

Stewards hate change and, therefore, chaos. It threatens their position of leadership. Stability is a world in control. This, too, is a comfort for the follower.

Listens to a Steward speak. Whether George Bush, Leonid Brehznev, or Roger Stemple, their presentations frequently cite how we need to avoid chaos. (If I had a vote for each time George Bush put down chaos in a presentation, I'd be President of the United States!)

To avoid chaos, Stewards install controls—balancing feedback systems—to insure that the system stays on track. They are great believers in management by objectives and performance appraisal systems, even when their followers fail to use them appropriately. They establish goals based on existing knowledge, and demand that those goals be met, regardless of what has happened in real time.

Extensive use of balancing feedback to control memory saps the creativity out of an organization. Deviations from the accepted and expected are punished. The lack of change keeps the organization at its point in history. As with Hamlet, the result is often that the Steward runs the organization onto the rocks of history.

The Use of Power

I hope that you have been tallying up lists of names of those who have been termed Conquerors and those called Stewards. If so, you will see something remarkable. The traditional groupings have broken down. Autocratic vs. democratic, conservative vs liberal, demagogues vs. egalitarians—these distinctions collapsed during this analysis.

Stephen Jobs, Lee Iaccoca, Newt Gignrich, Ross Perot, Hillary Clinton, Che Guevarra, Mao Zedong and Ronald Reagan all stand arm in arm conquering their environments. Roger Stemple, Leonid Brezhnev, Hua Guofeng (Mao Zedong's first successor), and George Bush all worked hard to maintain history, to venerate and support an already existing system, fighting back change and evolution to a new order.

By jumping to the perspective of complex systems, the rules have changed. The old distinguishers are no longer important. The key principle by which leaders are traditionally grouped relates, ultimately, to control—the use of power to achieve one's ends. Traditionally, those who command what is to be done and enforce their command through fear and intimidation are grouped as authoritarians. Those who use reason, logic, and/or personal relationship to maintain their power are humanitarian. Douglas McGregor, of course, made the distinction of Theory X leaders and Theory Y leaders, a continuum of behaviors on power usage in decision making.

But many Conquerors use fear and intimidation to enforce their vision beyond the true believers, while others incorporate humanitarian approaches within their vision. Stewards demanding control of memory can be notorious in their use of autocratic methods. But as Paul Hersey and Ken Blanchard have shown with their situational leadership model, if the skills, knowledge, and motivation is there, the Steward can take comfort within the group and allow for more active decision making with the members.

If both types use power one way or another, power is no longer a distinguishing characteristic of leadership. Instead, the cutting edge is the use or abuse of empowerment. A brief history of the concept of empowerment will make this clear. With all that has been written about empowerment, it turns out that none of our most respected leaders practices it.

Empowerment was supposed to be the development of democracy in organizational structures. It meant allowing decisions to be made at the lowest organizational level possible. Empowered individuals were supposed to be allowed to determine their own best strategy and then implement that strategy.

The history of the concept of empowerment is very illuminating. Although early precedents to the concept of empowerment can be found in the labor movement at the turn of the century, the term was first used in the civil rights movement. There, empowerment was not defined as entitlement being demanded but as an individually chosen action needing to be released. It was the sense that power was in the self. From there we see the concept describing the activities of individuals coming together voluntarily to achieve change within the nonprofit sector. Volunteers had better be empowered to make decisions or they will have no incentive to volunteer. Only when the concept was translated into the corporate environment in the 1980s did it become a top down management strategy to achieve management goals.

I had an interesting experience that convinced me that empowerment has not been realized in our organizations. I was giving a presentation to supervisors at US West Communications. It was my old chaos talk. Everything was going great. Heads were nodding up and down, there was eye contact. All of the signs that a speaker looks for to know that he is on target with the audience were there. Then I mentioned empowerment.

It was done very innocently. Theoretically, empowerment enables individuals to act based upon local rules and local conditions—the basic ingredients of self-organization. However, when I mentioned the word, everyone's eyes glazed over. It was so bad I had to stop and ask what was wrong. The answer, "Has anyone told you what empowerment means at US West?" I said no and asked for more. The speaker explained, "Empowerment means doing what your boss's boss wants your boss to do but your boss doesn't want to do."

Empowerment does not work so long as there is a vision. It does not matter whether the vision is of a new future or of a distant past. So long as there is the need to achieve that mission or to maintain memory, the leader must, ultimately use some form of power.

The success of the Conqueror or Steward rests on that leader's ability to garner support for the vision throughout the organization. This is the process of achieving alignment. It is managed by managing the organization's culture.

Authoritarians achieve alignment by using the power of position, rightness, or abuse to insure support. It is an easier task than for the humanitarian who must use persuasion and, often, manipulation to achieve his ends.

Humanitarians achieve alignment through training, culture management, and little vision cards carried in back pockets. These strategies insure that any decision made by an individual will be in accordance with the overall direction of the organization. So long as alignment exists there can only be something that appears to be "empowerment."

The flaw that gives a lie to this being true empowerment is the dreaded performance appraisal. At the very least, if an individual is guilty of making decisions that do not fall within the general alignment of the leader's vision, it will show up on the performance evaluation. From there it will show up in the next paycheck. The humanitarian has resorted to coercive means to achieve his/her ends. This is not true empowerment.

The Ritz-Carlton Hotel chain, which is headed by a Conqueror, demonstrates this so-called empowerment. The Ritz Carlton in Buckhead (Atlanta) was the winner of the Baldrige Award in 1992. Management prides itself on empowering each employee, who can spend as much as $500.00 to resolve a guest complaint without having to ask for permission from a supervisor. The company loves to share stories of employees who traveled great distances to find a special food or piece of clothing needed by a guest.

The Buckhead Ritz-Carlton's mission statement states that the hotel wants to be the quality and market leader of hotels. To achieve this, each department has its own mission statement. These statements used to assess performance, further the creation of a strict alignment for the hotel.

The new employee selection and orientation process augments the assessment process. The selection process is very structured. Entry requirements initially weed out those whose educational, personality, and/or work experience history suggests that they may not be comfortable within this rigid corporate alignment. Contrarians need not apply.

The orientation training is very intense for new employees, almost to a level reminiscent of a revival meeting. The company president appears at the start and end of the weeklong program, serving as both the premier practitioner of the company's values and as a father figure. The training is used to inculcate appreciation of the "Founders Of Our Principles:" "The Basics", "The Credo", "The Gold Standards", "The Three Steps of Service", and "The Motto," which, together, define the culture and management's expectations of employee behavior. There is a right of passage following the orientation program (graduation) into a probationary period.

During this second training phase, the employee is closely monitored to insure conformity with both technical procedures and culture standards. Only those passing the second right of passage are fully inducted into the family.

Many of us watching a presentation on the Ritz-Carlton's practices were taken aback by the almost propagandist nature of the orientation process. There was little difference in our minds between the brainwashing strategies of religious cults that produced zombie-like followers and the intensive behavior reinforcement strategies of the program. Combined with the company's database of preferences concerning its guests, the resulting feeling for us as visitors went beyond comfort to an almost Orwellian intensity.[95]

Of course, Ritz-Carlton staff can be empowered to make decisions, there is almost no chance for them to make a wrong decision following such an invasive orientation process!

Some of us did try to ask individual employees about what constitutes a mistake by the company, or can result in discipline. However, unfortunately, the staff was uncommunicative about such matters. This, clearly is not the empowerment that was meant by those professing the concept in the 1980s.

True empowerment and corporate vision/mission are completely incompatible concepts. So long as the leader requires conformance to a vision, whether a new one of the future or one dredged up from the past, the leader will be forced, at times, to coerce others into supporting that vision. Such coercion may be friendly persuasion or may be done at gunpoint, it is still an exercise of direct power.

In unions, the civil rights movement, and voluntary nonprofit organizations, empowerment is a function of the participant's free will. The volunteer joins in as an act of empowerment. Free will, not financial or other forms of coercion, leads the follower towards agreement with the hopes and purposes of the organization. Alignment develops through self-organization, directly from the membership process. If significant disagreement develops, the individual leaves freely as another act of empowerment.

---

95 The company's presentation answered an eerie experience I had on arrival. After check-in, at the insistence of the front desk clerk, a bellhop took me to my room. During our discussions, he surprisingly knew something about the topic I'd be presenting on - complexity theory. And we talked about his gayness and my brother's passing away from AIDS. The whole time I had a deja vu feeling, like I'd done this before. In fact, I had had a similar conversation with my bellhop at the Boston Ritz Carlton three years before! Had they retained that information in their database and prepped my new bellhop before I came?

The individual can never be coerced under these circumstances (unless brainwashed) because his/her survival (in terms of food and other goods) is not at stake. As a corollary, there is rarely a problem with motivation, especially in newly founded nonprofit organizations, since there is no dis-congruence between the individual's interests and that of the group's.

If empowerment is a real goal for an organization, then organizations must find some way to emulate the conditions found in voluntary organizations. They must find a way to end the need for coercion. The only way this can be achieved is by eliminating the function of vision and allowing for fluid memory.

Once vision is eliminated, all participants can focus on the fitness of the organization. Self-interest, skills, and abilities define the attractors for self-organization around the purpose. The results are never completely institutionalized so as to allow continued adaptation as the requirements of fitness change. The use of skill banks and project management strategies is pioneering efforts in creating such fluid organizations.

The role of the leader in the past has always been tied to the notion of vision. If we are to eliminate vision as a leadership function, we come to the great question of this book:

What is leadership without vision?

The Explorer

There is a subtle but important difference between a Conqueror and Explorer. Both require courage in the face of the unknown. Both seek out new territory not knowing if existing rules still apply. Both create new opportunities.

The Conqueror walks into the New World and attempts to mold it to meet his/her desires. S/he sees the new land as one to be tamed, rebuilt in his/her image. His/her vision is to transform the world into his/her image.

If a Steward happens to end up in virgin territory, he ignores what is new. Instead, he uses the New World's resources to serve his existing world. When he is done, he calls the New World "civilized."

The Explorer enters new territory to learn. The "Prime Objective" described in the Star Trek series—not to take any action that interferes with the natural development of the indigenous culture—describes how the Explorer likes to function. Yet, like Captain Kirk, the Explorer knows that this does not always work, because even observation may affect the observed, creating a co-evolutionary loop. The Explorer observes, learns, and attempts to adapt into the new environment, all the while experiencing some transformation himself.[96]

One is tempted to say that the Explorer gains insight into the New World. To the extent that learning about the New World requires stripping away the outer layers of false perception as a scientist might do, the word insight is appropriate.

The psychologist, James Hillman gives us a hint that insight may not be enough, however. Psychotherapy is a method for gaining insight into oneself. It is a journey inward. Likewise, the psychotherapist gains

---

96 If you are a Star Trek fan, you may realize that the difference between Explorers and Conquerors may be exemplified by observing the difference between the role of the Enterprise to seek out new civilizations...., and that of Clingons who apparently wish to conquer the universe.

A number of people have suggested a comparison between the Explorer and Joseph Campbell's description of the Hero. This is not an accurate comparison. The Hero goes to an unknown land, is transformed by the journey, takes something from that land and returns home to transform home. The Explorer as described here moves into the new land and makes a home of the new land. He cannot return home because the return route is blocked by the uni-directional arrow of time.

insight into the patient by guiding the patient inward. Using the term insight would imply such a role for the Explorer. But Hillman rightly complains that the process of psychotherapy is flawed. It fails to explore the relationship between the patient and his environment. When the psychotherapist and patient explore this larger world, what may at first appear irrational behavior can turn out to be a very rational adaptation to environmental realities.[97]

The Explorer practices holsight. In Chapter 4, holsight was defined as viewing and understanding the interrelationships existing in the here and now, particularly from a systems perspective. A core understanding from holsight is fitness. By understanding fitness, one brings aspects of a system, which are not responding to current needs, into the forefront of consideration. The process improves fitness—the ability to survive in the unknown environment.

Holsight is also fluid. Adapting to existing conditions changes those conditions. The fitness landscape changes. In response, the Explorer senses change and continues to adapt as necessary. This phenomenon is similar to a ship's captain's ability to sense problems with his ship even before visible symptoms of those problems emerge.

Both Conquerors and Stewards serve as the key conduit of information between the organization and the environment. True, modern management has evolved somewhat in this sense by making organizations more information permeable. This is an evolutionary response to information overload. It has lead to the development of total quality improvement and customer service emphasis being moved into the organization. These developments represent a movement towards leadership holsight and are not a part of the older management order. But

---

97 Hillman, James and Ventura, Michael, *We've Had A Hundred Years of Psychotherapy And The World's Still Getting Worse.*

in and of themselves, both total quality management and service management are limited in their capacity to maintain fitness.

Holsight requires effective tuning of sensors. One person cannot keep track of all that goes on within a system. An Explorer knows that having scouts increases the ability to prepare for change at the next bend in the river. With the development of information system infrastructures like the Internet and Intranets, it has become possible to make everyone a scout. Virtually any member of an organizational community may now have something to contribute to the decision making process of an organization.

Because I had started using white water rafting as a metaphor for chaos theory, some collaborators and I set out to try it on a river outside Pittsburgh. As novices, we had to go through a short training session before we were allowed into the river. There was one instruction that was repeated over and over again. When in heavy white water, "paddle or die." Everyone had to participate, there was no leader, and definitely no vision.[98]

The lack of vision coupled with the need for survival turns the Explorer's head away from concern for achieving a future state of being. The Explorer neither knows where the path will lead, nor will s/he predict its direction. S/he's more concerned with keeping the raft upright through the rapids, then what s/he'll face at their end. The Explorer emphasizes process, the here and now, and how the system is functioning, instead of output.

---

98 My co-explorers that day were two fine consultants, Lisa Marshall and Sandy Mobley, as well as Lisa's family friend. They tell the story a little differently. They agree about the training. But they add that we were told that if someone in the boat did not paddle, the person should be thrown out. Lisa goes on to say that throughout the ride, I kept making associations between what was happening and chaos theory. It got so bad, she claims, that they had to threaten me with a dunking before I shut up and paddled.

The Explorer promotes learning. Learning requires the ability to forget. When something new becomes known, the Explorer will help the group understand the experience in light of what is already known whenever possible. The system will be adjusted, not just dismantled. Older processes, which still work, will continue to function.

During the 1980s, many traditional manufacturing companies started experiencing bottlenecks in their inventory and process control functions as the demands for adaptable system outputs increased. The traditional assembly line systems were reaching their capacity to produce. The problem's source was the same as the self-organizing process which causes traffic jams on highways, solitons. The situation was comparable to Dupont's problem increasing the speed of the filmmaking machine described in Chapter 2.

As happens in creative developments, a number of companies experimented with new production methods. They were searching for a new level of fitness. Eventually, the notion of work cells emerged. Work cell technology involves restructuring the assembly line into compact assembly systems where a team handles a group of production steps at one site instead of the product moving from site to site and individual to individual. The linear function was broken down into smaller, nonlinear processes.

Conversion to work cells did not require firing all the current employees. Instead, they received cross training on other pieces of equipment. It turned out that they did not even need training in teamwork, which evolved as a natural adaptation of behavior associated with the conversion. The change did not require getting rid of all the equipment. While some new equipment was needed, mostly equipment just had to be moved around. This adaptation process is a prime example of associative learning by an organization.

The Explorers who experienced success with work cells shared their information with others. They opened the New World to further exploration. Moreover, as with most innovations in business, the process succeeded for those who were ready for it, but failed for those who were not ready. Those companies that did not have the volume of work representing a need for change that changed on the whim of a fad, found that they did not reduce their costs or production time as a result of the change. We have to know a chair before we can understand a sofa.

The Explorer thrives to keep the organization at the edge of chaos. In other words, s/he sees that the organization maintains an underlying current of weak chaos. We have described weak chaos as the ongoing, effect of experiencing natural change in an organization. Weak chaos comes from diversity within the organization, acceptance that change goes on outside the organization, and, most importantly, establishing a spirit to adapt to the changes affecting the organization, rather than resisting those changes.

The notions of weak chaos and learning through association work hand in hand. Weak chaos is the nature of information and energy coming into the system and within the system. Association is the mode of ongoing adaptation to that information. As we saw in the discussion of learning, even learning within the brain is a weakly chaotic process.

The Explorer establishes and maintains the infrastructure necessary to maintain an ongoing current of weak chaos. At a minimum that includes

- an employee selection process that insures a diverse workforce,
- a communications structure that facilitates sharing of successes across intra-organizational boundaries,
- a culture that supports honesty, risk taking, creativity, and diverse ideas
- facilitation of conflict rather than conflict resolution.

There is no need for a power relationship between the Explorer and the followers. The Explorer has nothing to control that would need such a relationship. Without vision, there is no need to continue in a planned direction when the path curves. Nor is there a need to enforce alignment to the vision, since diversity is valued over any vision as the key to survival. Purpose survives as the general organizing principle. Alignment becomes the natural result of self-organization. Alignment changes fluidly as the landscape requires.

The Explorer leads through real empowerment, the ability of each to take individual action as needed. In short, empowerment is recognition of the idea of paddle or die. So long as almost everyone buys into that responsibility and an effective infrastructure is built, the organization becomes an adaptive system, ready to meet the most demanding challenges of the wilderness.

The notion of the Explorer as leader, at least as identified here, is new. Clearly, no one has purposely lead in the manner of an Explorer. In hindsight, I have identified individuals who have the markings of Explorer behavior.

Pope John XXIII was an explorer. He led an organization that was losing members because it had lost touch with its potential market. People could not understand the values of the Catholic Church because everything was spoken in a foreign tongue. Had he been a Conqueror, Pope John would have attempted to revolutionize the Church. He was in a position to command obedience to a vision of a new religious order that fit the needs of modern Catholics. Had he been a Steward, the Church would have continued its descent into the quagmire.

Instead, Pope John opened up the change process to the members. He created an ecumenical and ecclesiastical conference, which included representatives from throughout the Church. He asked them to define change, rather than asking them to support his changes. He could not know where things would end. It was an amazing act of faith.

Mikhail Gorbechev oversaw the dismantling of the Soviet Union. As a communist, this was certainly not his intended vision. But he, too, saw the need for change. In doing so, he also recognized that he was only one of many explorers.

Gorbechev instituted Glasnost to open the process up in a way, which allowed a diversity of opinions. Gorbechev hoped that the result would be to reach what he felt would be a logical conclusion, instituting a more enlightened communism. But the system had been under such strong control for so long that the diversity exploded into endless opportunities for change that could not be contained. Swarming took over the Soviet Union.

Gorbechev had the options of both the Conqueror and the Steward. He could have attempted to institute a new communism by fiat, or he could have crushed the democratic movements. Instead, Gorbechev decided to allow the process to continue and, eventually, relinquish the power available to him. His bravery was the likely reason why the Soviet Union did not blow up in what could have been world ending violence. The most telling sign of his role as Explorer, as one who recognizes the vanity of personal power relative to the awesomeness of natural change, was his private statement right before his farewell address to the nation, "When it is time to go, it is time to go."

Deng Xiaoping, China's top leader following Mao Zedong's death, may also have been an Explorer. As a reformer, he worked to open up the economic and market systems to interface with the rest of the world, yet still keeping one eye on memory. The unfortunate result was the massacre at Tianeman Square, a blemish that makes one consider Xiaoping a Steward of the worst kind. However, the incident was not followed by a drastic increase in oppression, and the Chinese government continued to open its borders to its environment. With the inclusion of Hong Kong into the People's Republic, the society is reaching another decision point in which the outcomes will be either further democratization or extreme repression to root out the reform that threatens the current leaders. In the future, Tianeman Square may be viewed more as comparable to Lech Walesa jumping over the fence at the Gdansk shipyard, then as a revolution crushed.

Jack Welch at GE and Lou Gerstner at IBM, represent the growth of Explorer style leaders in the US business community. Welch likely was not born an explorer. He is a strong believer in controls, in setting goals and seeing them achieved. However, in the late 1980s, he instituted a meeting process that he called "Workouts". Workouts are very empowering. They provide an institutionalized opportunity for employee input. Managers and Welch directly received information that had alluded them. This information is quickly turned to action and change. The workout does not appear to be dependent upon a vision. More importantly, it established a method by which the organization could open up to additional sources of information, and turns that information into quick change.

When Lou Gerstner took over at IBM, the company was falling apart. It was losing money and market share. For weeks the press asked Mr. Gerstner what his vision was for the future of IBM, but he refused to answer. Gerstner did not want to be tied to a vision. He was busy meeting with managers and staff trying to facilitate decisions, which would lead to a turnaround of the company's fortunes. But the questions persisted, because investors place their bets based on their agreement with the leader's vision. Finally, one day he told a reporter in exasperation, "If IBM must have a vision, then its first frame damn well better be to make a profit."

Through these actions, Gerstner demonstrated that he recognized that the issue was not one of vision, but one of survival. He knew the landscape had changed and would continue to change. He served as the infrastructure to enable the flow of ideas, projects, and experiments that could lead to the rebirth of the company.

When Gerstner took the reins at IBM, the stock had plummeted from its traditional high of around 100 down to the 40's range. As of this writing, IBM hovers around its all time high of 105, following a stock split during 1997. The landscape for computer equipment has never stopped evolving. The question remains whether IBM under Gerstner's leadership will continue to evolve with it.

Conclusion

Ecclesiastics, the Preacher said, "To everything there is a season… And behold, there is nothing new under the sun." The Preacher saw a world of cycles, of repetition, of birth, death, and renewal. His image was appropriate for a world in which the sun, moon and stars circled the earth, a world in which change was just a wisp of imagination. The Preacher adhered to the second of our creation stories.

Since then, we have learned that our universe is vast; we are not at its center; and we are likely not alone in it. We have learned that cycles exist at one level of reality, but that within the larger universe, there is a single directional arrow of time. What has gone before cannot be repeated. In response to the new creation story, we are all becoming Explorers on the path of time. Each has but a moment on the path, together we will only be but a flash.

Because we are all Explorers, in some way we are all leaders. In the past this has been a challenge. As my vision interferes with yours, you attack in fear of your loss. Our way to resolve this conflict was to envision a single unified world—one culture, one people, one earth. (We even hoped for an invasion of aliens to help bring this about.)

Through the emerging new sciences we are gaining a new understanding of these relationships. We have learned that long term survival of the gene pool requires maintaining diversity within that pool. Sex evolved as a way to maintain that diversity, and sex is the process of breaking up symmetry, not creating it. We have learned that 99% of all species that have lived on this earth are now extinct. This sounds like the notion that 90% of all new companies fail. Yet families, such as the dinosaurs, learned to evolve by maintaining diversity—differences, within their species, resulting in their evolution when needed. The key to survival is diversity. It is unity, oneness, sameness that is our enemy

Organizations are complex systems operating the same as ecological systems and complex chemical systems. They follow the same inherent rules. The logical application of these rules suggests a new approach to organizations and leadership. We explored seven of those rules in Chapter 2. Applying the rules led to understanding that fitness, not vision—is needed in the here and now for survival. Emphasis on fitness leads to understanding the landscape on which we dwell and being able to adapt to changes in that landscape. By applying the basics of complexity theory, we learned that maintaining a diversity of ideas is the key to such adaptation, and not achieving unity through control.

This change in perspective places us firmly in our role as a participant in history and nature, rather than as outside of both. It turns out that it is nature itself, in the form of self-organization, that provides the real controls, establishes the unity through system relationships.

As Explorers in this universe, we are much more likely to take wonder at all that is around us. We are much more likely to respect all that is around us. We are much more likely to act in concert with our surroundings.

The same is true of our organizational life. As Explorers, we stay prepared for the unexpected small catastrophes like market downturns or technological advancements. Our focus improves when we stress maintaining diversity, flexibility, and permeability as our primary resources for survival.

We also never lose sight of the potentially devastating catastrophe. We are aware that eventually, our organization may run out of steam, merge or die, and that this is the natural order of life. Our knowledge of the large catastrophe keeps us aware that we are just sojourners, just explorers on the arrow of time.

Bibliography

Armstrong, Karen. *A History of God: The 4000 Year Quest of Judaism, Christianity and Islam.* Knopf Publishers, 1993

Arthur, W. Brian. "Positive Feedback in the Economy" *Scientific American*, February 1990

Bak, Per and Chen, Kan. "Self-Organized Criticality." *Scientific American*, January 1991

Boslough, John. *Stephen Hawkins Universe.* New York: William Morrow and Company, 1985

Cassidy, John. "The Force of an Idea" *The New Yorker Magazine* Jan 12, 1998

Casti, John L. *Paradigms Lost: Images of man in the mirror of science.* New York: William Morrow and Company, 1989

Caudill, Maureen and Butler,Charles. *Naturally Intelligent Systems.* Cambridge, MA: MIT Press, 1990

de Geus, Arie. *The Living Organization.* Boston: Harvard Business School Press, 1997

Ferris, Timothy. *The Whole Shebang: A state-of-the-universe(s) report.* Simon & Schuster, 1997

Glance, Natalie S. and Huberman, Bernardo A. "Chaos and Cooperation" in Albert, A. *Chaos and Society.* IOS Press, 1995

Gleick, James. *Chaos: The making of a new science.* Penguin Books, 1987

Goldstein, Jeffrey. *The Unshackled Organization.* Portland: Productivity Press, 1994

Goldstein, Jeffrey. "A Far-From-Equilibrium Approach to Resistance to Change."*Organizational Dynamics* Vol. 17(2)

Gould, Stephen J. *Wonderful Life: The Burgess Shale and the Nature of History*. W. W. Norton & Company, 1990

Guastello, Stephen. *Chaos, Catastrophe, and Human Affairs: Applications of Nonlinear Dynamics to Work, Organizations, and Social Evolution.* Lawrence Erlbaum Associates, 1995

Hillman, John and Ventura, Michael. *We've Had a Hundred Years of Pschotherapy and the World's Still Getting Worse.* HarperSanFrancisco, 1992

Hof, Robert D. and Sager, Ira. "The Sad Saga of Silicon Graphics." *BusinessWeek* August 4, 1997

Holland, John H. *Hidden Order: How Adaptation Builds Complexity*. Addison Wesley, 1995

Hubler, Alfred. "The Control of Chaos" in Michaels, Mark, ed. *Proceedings of the 3rd Annual Chaos Network Conference*. Urbana, IL: People Technologies, 1992

Hurst, David. *Crisis and Renewal: Meeting the Challenge of Organizational Change.* Boston: Harvard Business School Press, 1995

Jaynes, Julian. *The Origin of Consciousness and the Breakdown of the Bicameral Mind.* Boston: Houghton Mifflin Co., 1976

Kauffman, Stuart. *At Home in the Universe.* Oxford University Press, 1995

Kellert, Stephen H. *In The Wake of Chaos.* University of Chicago Press, 1993

Kreidel, Robert. *Game Plans: Sports Strategies for Business.* E.P. Dutton, 1985

Lewin, Roger, *Complexity, Life on the Edge of Chaos.* New York: Macmillan Publishing Co., 1992

Michaels, Mark, "Thoughts on the 25th Anniversary of the Organization Development Institute" *The Organization Development Journal,* Vol. 11(2)

Michaels, Mark. "Chaos Theory and the Process of Change" in Cole, Donald W. et al, eds. *What's New in Organization Development*. The Organization Development Institute, 1994

Michaels, Mark. "The Beer Distribution Game: A Second Look". *The Chaos Network News*letter Vol 5 (1)

Minsky, Marvin. *The Society of Mind*. Touchstone Press, 1988

Mosekilde, Erik and Larsen, Erik Reimer. "Deterministic Chaos in the Beer Distribution Model." *System Dynamics Review* Vol 4(1)

Peters, Thomas J. and Waterman, Robert H. Jr. *In Search of Excellence: Lessons from America's Best Run Companies*. HarperCollins, 1982

Peters, Tom. *Thriving on Chaos: Handbook for a Management Revolution*. Alfred A. Knopf, 1987

Peters, Tom: *The Circle of Innovation: You Can't Shrink Your Company to Greatness*. Knopf Publishers, 1997

Priesmeyer, Richard, *Organizations and Chaos*. West Port CT: Quorum Books, 1992

Prigogine, Ilya. And Stengers, Isabelle. *The End of Certainty: Time, Choas and the New Laws of Nature*. The Free Press, 1997

Redding, John and Catalenello, Ralf. *Strategic Readiness: The Making of a Learning Organization*. San Francisco: Jossey Bass, 1994

Regis, Ed, "The Doom Slayer". *Wired Magazine* Vol. 5(2)

Restack, Richard. *The Brain*. Bantam Books, 1984

Roetzheim, William H. *The Complexity Lab: Where Chaos Meets Complexity*. Indianapolis: SAMS Publishing, 1994

Samuelson, Robert. "The Way the World Works" in *Newsweek*, January 12, 1998

Senge, Peter et al. *The Fifth Discipline Fieldbook*. Currency, Doubleday, 1994

Senge, Peter, *The Fifth Discipline: The art of the learning organization*. Curreny/Doubleday, 1990

Stacey, Ralph. *Complexity and Creativity in Organizations*. San Francisco: Berrett Koehler, 1996

Stacey, Ralph. *Managing the Unknowable*. San Francisco: Jossey-Bass, 1992

Toffler, Alvin, *The Third Wave*. Mass Marketing Paperback, 1991

Vaill, Peter B., *Managing as a Performing Art: New Ideas for a World of Chaotic Change*. Jossey-Bass, 1989

Waterman, Robert. *The Renewal Factor*. Bantam Books, 1988

Zimmerman, Brenda. "The Management of Boredom" in Michaels, Mark, ed. *The Second Iteration: Proceedings of the Chaos Netwrok Conference 1992*. Urbana, IL, People Technologies

Index

www.ingramcontent.com/pod-product-compliance
Lightning Source LLC
Chambersburg PA
CBHW030918180526
45163CB00002B/376